# ROMANS

*The Freedom Letter*

VOLUME 2

# ROMANS

*The Freedom Letter*

## VOLUME 2

Romans 8—16

*By*

ALAN F. JOHNSON

MOODY PRESS

CHICAGO

The two EBC volumes of Romans were originally published in
one volume under the title
*The Freedom Letter.*

© 1974 by
THE MOODY BIBLE INSTITUTE
OF CHICAGO

Everyman's Bible Commentary edition, 1976

ISBN: 0-8024-2064-8

7 8 9 10 11 12 Printing/LC/Year 87 86 85 84 83

Except where indicated otherwise, all scripture quotations in
this book are from the New American Standard Bible, used by
permission of THE LOCKMAN FOUNDATION, copyright 1960,
1962, 1963, 1971, 1973, all rights reserved.

The use of selected references from various versions of the
Bible in this publication does not necessarily imply publisher
endorsement of the versions in their entirety.

*Printed in the United States of America*

## THE BOOK OF ROMANS IN
## ONE SENTENCE

"What is man? Man is God's creature; Yes, but man is God's image, and through the misuse of his God-bestowed freedom, man is God's shame and man is God's problem; But by that incredible strategy of the cross, God makes it possible for man to become the Creator's child; And man may become the Creator's co-laborer, and man, finite man, may become the friend of an infinite and all-holy God; And ultimately man may be, if he will have it so, God's glory."

VERNON C. GROUNDS

# Contents

# Introduction

FROM CHAPTER 5 through chapter 8 of the book of Romans, Paul has been establishing the "new situation" in grace of those who stand acquitted before God. He has argued that they are not only forgiven but brought to a radically new relationship of life and righteousness before God through the grace which is in Christ (chap. 5). Paul has spoken to the twin moral problems of continued sin in the Christian's life (chap. 6) and the end of the dominance of the law for those who are in Christ (chap. 7). Finally, he has expounded the main principles of the new life in the Spirit as the counterpart of the old way of life under the law (chap. 8). In his final hymn of victory (8:31-39) Paul has sung his heart out in adoration to the unqualified faithfulness of God from which nothing can ever separate us.

This unshakable confidence in God's ability to keep his promises raises the final problem of the letter. "Paul," it might be asked, "didn't God make promises to the nation of Israel in the Old Testament? Doesn't your Gospel, as it has developed historically, show that God has rejected the Jew and thus broken His covenant to them?" The fact is that the majority of people in the nation of Israel are not believers in the Messiah. Paul's answer to this grave problem is given in the following section (Ro 9-11).

# Outline of Romans

# 1

## The New Life of the Spirit

### 8:1-39

THE SITUATION presented in chapter 8 is the contemporaneous but also the complementary side of Christian experience to that described in chapter 7. This new-life principle of the Spirit enables those who are justified in Christ ("no condemnation," v. 1): (1) to fulfill the moral law (v. 4); (2) to rise above the operating principle of sin and death (v. 2); and (3) to enjoy life and peace (v. 6). In this chapter Paul describes many of the gifts and graces of the Holy Spirit, who now enables the Christian to experience in part what he will have in full at Christ's return even though at the same time he experiences the frustrations he has which are described in chapter 7.

Romans chapter 8 is one of the greatest chapters in the Bible. If the Bible were a ring and Romans the jewel in the center, then chapter 8 would be the sparkling point of the jewel. Charles Erdman has splendidly captured the excitement of entering onto this holy ground:

> If the Epistle to the Romans rightly has been called "the cathedral of Christian faith," then surely the eighth chapter may be regarded as its most sacred shrine, or its high altar of worship, of praise, and of prayer. . . . Here, we stand in the full liberty of the children of God, and enjoy a prospect of that glory of God which some day we are to share.[1]

Truly spoken, for the chapter begins with "in Christ Jesus" (v. 1),

1. Charles Erdman, *The Epistle of Paul to the Romans* (Philadelphia: Westminster, 1925), p. 82.

13

and ends with "in Christ Jesus our Lord" (v. 39); it begins with *no condemnation* (v. 1) and ends with *no separation* (v. 39).

There are two main themes developed in the chapter. Both focus on the release from captivity which is effected by the Holy Spirit. First, verses 1-13 develop the thought of *release from the captivity of sin and death,* while *release from the captivity of decay* forms the main focus in verses 14-39. Both themes are closely related. The Spirit of God, whose power enables Christians to rise above the power of the sinful flesh and progress in sanctification (yet, not without constant struggles), is also the firstfruit guaranteeing their glorious future inheritance.

### RELEASE FROM THE CAPTIVITY OF SIN AND DEATH
### 8:1-13

Paul's long argument in vindication of the moral nature of the faith method of justification (6:1—7:25) now reaches its clearest and fullest statement in verses 1-13. Contrary to all the supposed objections, this method of justification was the only possible method by which sinful men could be completely forgiven and released from captivity to sin so that "the requirement of the Law might be fulfilled in us" (v. 4).

Paul first summarizes the former arguments of the book. He relates how we have been simultaneously freed from the wrath of God and freed from the captivity of sin by being made part of a new way of life which he describes as walking "not according to the flesh, but according to the Spirit" (v. 4).[2] This new life in the Spirit (v. 2) becomes possible by the appearance in human flesh of the Son of God who by His sinless life and sacrificial death doomed the rule of sin over human nature (v. 3). Jesus now gives birth to a new humanity of people who walk ˃ t according to the flesh but according to the rule of the indwelling Holy Spirit (vv. 4-14).

---

2. The words "who walk not after the flesh, but after the Spirit," found in the first verse in the KJV are omitted by most modern versions because a number of early Greek manuscripts omit them. The same words appear at the end of verse 4, suggesting that a scribe may have accidentally repeated the phrase in verse 1. However, there is strong manuscript support for the KJV reading, and it fits admirably into the context if we understand Paul's thought at this point in the argument.

In verse 1 Paul states in summary and recapitulation, "There is therefore now no condemnation for those who are in Christ Jesus." The "therefore now" probably goes back to 7:6 where, followed by a lengthy explanation of the holiness of the law and the sinfulness of human nature (7:7-25), Paul has stated that we are free from the law's condemning curse, which held us captive, and able now to serve God in the new life of the Spirit. Chapter 8 more fully explains this new life lived by the Holy Spirit. To not be under "condemnation"[3] refers both to justification as release from the wrath of God (chap. 5) and also to our release from the enslaving effect of the law and its curse (6:15–7:6). The Christian can really rejoice because in God's grace and mercy "in Christ Jesus" (in union with Him, 6:3-5) all of our sinfulness and rebellion against God has been forgiven. Our guilt, which was a part of our sinful flesh, has been abolished forever.

Paul states again for us in verses 2-4 why there is no longer servitude to the sinful flesh. It is simply because Christians have been released from the former way of life "in the flesh" by the invasion of a new principle (law) of life lived in obedience to the Spirit (v. 2). How did this new manner of life come to us? It was made available totally through God's own gracious, saving act in the coming and the death of His Son (vv. 3-4). Jesus entered into the world by fully identifying Himself with the sinful human flesh He came to redeem: "in the likeness of sinful flesh" (v. 3). Yet it should be stressed that "likeness" of sinful flesh means neither that Christ was sinful (see 2 Co 5:21; 1 Pe 2:22), nor that He only appeared to be human, but that He came in real human flesh which "looked like" every other person since Adam (sinful flesh) but was different because He, unlike other men, was not under sin's dominion. Christ came "for sin" that is, to deal with sin or to offer Himself as a sin offering (3:24-25; 1 Jn 4:10).

Ultimately the purpose of His coming was to condemn "sin in the flesh" (v. 3). The law, by mere commanding, could not over-

3. "Condemnation" (Gr. *katakrima*) when God is the subject refers both to the sentence of judgment and to the execution of that sentence (TDNT). This same word occurs in 5:12-14 as indicating the actual condition of men in Adam, involving them in servitude to sin, disobedience to God, and death. To be removed from these is justification which is more than mere acquittal; it involves also being "set free from the law of sin and death" (v. 2).

come the practice of sin in human nature. It could prescribe the
will of God but provided no power for performing His will in
face of the sinful flesh. Yet it was not the law's fault that sin
prevailed and even increased under its rule. The failure lay in
the "weakness" of the law to effect righteousness in us because sin
ruined our flesh, making it powerless to respond (7:7-25). But
now God has done what the law wanted to do but could not do.
He has condemned the rule of sin over human nature by creating
a new humanity for mankind in Jesus Christ. By living a fully
human life, totally in obedience to God, Jesus broke the rule that
sin had held over human nature ever since Adam. He showed sin
to be not natural to humanness but a usurper. By His own death
Christ provided the means whereby all who are related to Him
can also enter into His same victory over the rule of sin (6:2-14).

This same thought is now repeated in verse 4, where Paul says
that Christ condemned sin in the flesh "in order that the requirement[4] of the Law might be fulfilled in us." The requirement of
the law was that we should be holy before God. The whole law,
Jesus said, is fulfilled in this, "You shall love the Lord your God ...
your neighbor as yourself" (Lk 10:27; Ro 13:9). Loving obedience both to God and to men was the holy aim in many of the
law's commands.

However, in actual human experience, the law was not able
to produce loving obedience because of the sin-controlled flesh.
But now the believer in Christ has this just goal of the law fulfilled in him due to the simple fact that in Christ he is no longer
living unto himself. Through union with Christ by faith, the
Christian has entered into a whole new way of life. He lives according to the rule and resources of the Holy Spirit of God rather
than the resources of the flesh. This change in relationship is captured well in the following:

> To run and work the law commands,
> Yet gives me neither feet nor hands;
> But better news the gospel brings:
> It bids me fly, and gives me wings.
> AUTHOR UNKNOWN

4. This is the same word (Gk. *dikaiōma*) discussed at 1:32; 2:26; 5:16, 18.
The closest parallel is 2:26 where it means "righteous demand or requirement."

The law of the Spirit of life in Christ Jesus (v. 2) is described in verse 4 as walking not "according to the flesh, but according to the Spirit." In verses 5-14 Paul shows what is involved in this new way of living in the Spirit.

But what then becomes of the Mosaic law for the believer in Christ? Does verse 4 teach that the Christian is enabled by the Holy Spirit to keep all the commands which he could not keep as a non-Christian and thus to fulfill the law? *No!* Christians cannot keep the law perfectly either. The point is that the law demanded obedience to God motivated out of love for God. This demand is met through the gospel for those who by the grace of God have been put into a whole new relationship to God through Christ. This is what Paul is stressing. That the Christian will be sensitive to any revealed expression of God's will, including the Mosaic commands, is assumed by Paul, but law-keeping is not the Christian's chief concern. Instead he is to focus on the "new life of the Spirit" (7:6; 8:5-14), not on the old written code. (See 13:8-10 for more on this point.)

Paul now turns to explain this life lived according to the Spirit (vv. 5-14). The Spirit comes to us as a gift (not merited in any way) when we become Christians. Through this gift God's love was poured out into the hearts of Christians (5:6). In 7:6 the Spirit is referred to as the agent of the new life. Jesus Christ is our justification and our sanctification, and it is the Holy Spirit who makes Him real and effective to us from day to day. The "Spirit of God" and "Spirit of Christ" appear to be identical terms (v. 9). So justification can never be separated from sanctification (Christ-likeness). Both are inseparably linked to the grace-gift of God in Jesus Christ. Yet how does the Spirit in our experience effect sanctification?

First, the Holy Spirit produces in us a certain mind-set (vv. 5-8): "those who are according to the Spirit [set their minds on (Gk. *phroneo*, are intent on following)] the things of the Spirit" (v. 5). It may be helpful to note that certain terms Paul uses here denote either different states of existence (Christian or non-Christian) or different patterns of behavior. To be "in the flesh" is to be a non-Christian, under sin's power (vv. 8, 9); on the other hand, to be "in the Spirit" or "in Christ" is to be a Christian, under the Spirit's power. To "walk according to the flesh" is equivalent to "to live according to the flesh" or be "according to the flesh" and means to conduct our lives according to the standard, values, and resources of the sin-dominated flesh (vv. 5, 12, 13). On the other hand, to "walk according to the Spirit" is equivalent to "according to the Spirit" and "by the Spirit you are putting to death the deeds of the body," and means to conduct our lives according to the standard, values, and resources of the life-giving Spirit within us (vv. 4, 5, 13).[5] The presence of the Holy Spirit redirects our life toward God and creates in us new desires and values. To "set the mind on" the things of the flesh or Spirit means to have one's thoughts, desires, and constant yearning directed toward either the life of the flesh (self) or the life of the Spirit (Christ).

The results follow (v. 6). To have one's mind directed only upon the things of self and this material world means cutting oneself off from the only Source of real human life and results in death now in this life (condemnation and evil) and eternal death to come.[6] On the other hand, to have one's mind directed upon God through the Spirit results in "life" (acquittal and sanctification) and "peace," the conscious enjoyment of reconciliation with God.

Paul further describes the mind directed onto the flesh (non-Christian) in its relationship to God (vv. 7-8). The flesh's interests are such that those who live to please themselves are in fact in a state of hostility against God. Such hostility is evident because the mind directed by the sinful flesh does not and cannot become obedient to the law (will) of God (7:14-25). It follows then that such who live to please themselves cannot live to please God.

The opposite then would be true of those who have been put by grace into the mind directed by the Spirit: instead of disobedience to the law (will) of God there is loving obedience; in place of walking apart from God there is walking with God.

5. It is also possible to be "walking" *in* the flesh (as a weak human being) but not "warring *after* the flesh" (i.e., drawing on the resources, standards, and values of sinful flesh). See 2 Co 10:2-3.

6. "The mind" (*phronēma*) set "on the things of the flesh" is the noun form of the same verb used for "mind" in v. 5.

In verses 9-11 Paul contrasts the state of the Christian ("in the Spirit") with the preceding description of those "in the flesh" (vv. 7-8). In verse 9, "however you," the "you" is emphatic: "but as for *you*." Paul clearly teaches in verse 9 that all Christians are "in the Spirit," which means that "the Spirit of God dwells" in every Christian. In fact, he says, "if anyone does not have the Spirit of Christ, he does not belong to Him" (as a justified one). To be "in Christ" or "in the Spirit" refers to our union with Christ; to have Christ in us (v. 10) or the Spirit in us (v. 4) refers to our ownership by Christ.

The Spirit "dwells" (Gk. *oikeō*, to live in a house) in us in the sense of a person making his home in our lives. The figure of indwelling combines the thought that Christians are people whose lives are directed from a Source outside themselves with the idea that this life Source is also vitally related to them. Three times in verses 9-11 this indwelling of the Spirit is stressed.

What are the effects in our experience of this indwelling Spirit of God? Paul states that, even though the body is dead due to sin, the Spirit is alive because of righteousness (v. 10). What he teaches is a modified dualism in Christian experience. At the present time there is a dual principle operating in the Christian. On the one hand, he still possesses a physical body condemned to death because of Adam's sin (5:15; 6:23). The seed of decay and death is now working in our bodies. Yet for the Christian there is also now another reality at work. Life is also present due to the indwelling of the Spirit given to us through justification. The Spirit enables us to "live" in spite of the fact that the body has been stricken with a death wound (v. 13).[7] The Christian then, while still in the weak, sinful flesh, has been released from its power; while still in the body, which has received a mortal wound from sin, he has a new principle of life working in it through the righteousness of God in Christ. He is totally dead on the one hand, yet fully alive on the other. Such a truth will spare us from

7. Most interpreters have understood the word "spirit" in verse 10 as a contrast to the "body" and refer it to the human "spirit" rather than the Holy Spirit (NASB, "the spirit is alive"). The objection to this latter view is simply that the Holy Spirit is the subject of the whole context and is immediately connected in v. 11 with life (see John Murray, *The Epistle to the Romans*, 294; C. K. Barrett, *The Epistle to the Romans*, p. 162; Anders Nygren, *Commentary on Romans*, p. 326).

either expecting absolute perfection in this life or giving in to complete pessimism concerning the present manifestation of Christ's love and righteousness in our lives.

Furthermore, the presence of the same Spirit, who gives life now to believers living in decaying bodies, also is the guarantee that our bodies, destined to physical death, will be raised from death in the same manner that Jesus' body was raised (v. 11). The Father is the specific agent in resurrection as in the case of Christ (6:4), but as in Christ's case, the Holy Spirit also is an agent (1:4). Later in the chapter Paul will again refer to this future hope of resurrection as the "redemption of our body" (v. 23). Here again we are reminded that just as human nature was not made for sin but the usurper illegally took it over (v. 3), so also the mortal body was not made for death and will be in God's time, because of the Spirit of life, raised to immortal life (1 Co 15:51-53). This is no mere spiritual resurrection. What a glorious truth!

But what about the life now in the body? Has the Spirit nothing to contribute? How does the "life" made possible because of our justification (v. 10) actually manifest itself in our deathbound lives? Paul has already said that the Christian as a Christian is one who walks not according to the flesh but after the Spirit (vv. 4-14). But does this mean that Christians now, since they are "in the Spirit," automatically follow God's will? The answer must be no, for in verses 12-14 Christians are specifically exhorted to "live according to the Spirit." Remember in  chapter 6 how Paul stated that because of his union with Christ in death and resurrection the believer was "free from sin" and then he proceeded to exhort them to fight against sin and yield themselves as servants to righteousness? Delivered and yet not delivered. Here likewise the Christian has been shown to be ultimately free from death (vv. 11, 21), due to the Spirit who indwells, but he must in the present life fight the sin and death principle as it works itself out in our bodies.

To live according to the flesh (in separation from God) leads to death both now and eternally. Since Christians have been removed from the servitude to the flesh (self) and put into the service of the Spirit, who is the Spirit of life and immortality, they are obligated (morally) not to live their lives under the rule of the sinful flesh. Rather, Christians are to "put to death the deeds of the body" that they might live (v. 13). Here is the principle for moving into the practice of holy living. It may be called spiritual neurosurgery. Phillips' translation reads: "cut the nerve of your instinctive actions by obeying the Spirit." "Putting to death the deeds of the body" refers to our continual (present tense) activity as Christians whereby, through the enablement provided by the Spirit, we strike down in death those sinful practices of the body which are contrary to God's will.

More specifically, how this is done Paul does not say in this context. The "deeds (habits) of the body" are probably to be identified with the "members of your earthly body" of Colossians 3:5 which are enumerated as: "immorality, impurity, passion, evil desire, and greed, which amounts to idolatry" (see also Gal 5:19-21; Eph 4:22—5:14).

While in this context the spiritual neurosurgery is primarily negative, it assumes that the process is a *renewal*, not simply a destruction. The dead leaves and branches of the sinful practices fall away only to make room for the "fruit of the Spirit" (6:21; 7: 4; Gal 5:22-23). The weed-killer of the Spirit is applied so that the grass of the graces of God might be free to grow. So in practice we do not seek mere patience or love or purity (this is a moralistic approach), but we seek the release of Christ's life, i.e., His patience, His love and purity by following the promptings of the Spirit. The Christian life is an exchanged life. Such a process leads truly to "life" now as well as eternal and immortal life in the future.

Verse 14 is transitional. Paul concludes the thought of the previous verses by asserting that all who are thus "being led by the Spirit of God [to be constantly putting to death the deeds of the body], these are the sons of God." The truth of the Spirit's leading suggests not general guidance as to what God would have us to do (vocation) but rather what we should be (character). All the children of God enjoy this leading; however, it is not optional. Since "leading" often implies the process whereby our desires lead us (2 Ti 3:6), perhaps the thought of Paul is that the Holy Spirit imparts new desires and promptings into the redeemed life to which the Christian develops a sensitivity in responding both negatively (killing process) and positively (in the fruit bearing process).

"Sons" of God includes being children of God but also involves in the Roman world of Paul's day the idea of a new mature stage in the child's development that relates him to his father as a joint heir and master over all (Gal 3:26; 4:6-7). So Paul will turn now to the thought of the future inheritance (vv. 17-18) as soon as he has given evidence to assure his readers that they truly are "sons."

### RELEASE FROM THE CAPTIVITY OF DECAY
#### 8:15-39

The Spirit, who now relates to us in a new way of life even though we are still in the old human sin nature (vv. 1-14), is also the "spirit of adoption" (v. 15). The Spirit's presence in us now is the "first fruits" (v. 23) of the future deliverance of the entire creation from the bondage of decay (v. 21). It is this assurance of sonship and heirship that the Holy Spirit constantly bears home to us in the Scripture and in our hearts that constitutes Christian hope. Hope leads us to patient endurance even through suffering and persecution (vv. 18-39). This section of the chapter is one of the most beautiful, triumphant, and comforting portions of the whole Bible.

Verses 15-17 continue the thought of the preceding verse by stressing assurance that as Christians we are actually related to God as "sons" and not as those under "slavery." Fear comes from the absence of authentic hope and leads to enslavement by inferior earthly powers which promise deliverance. But Christians have been made true sons of God (adopted)[8] and possess the assurance of genuine hope. The evidence of this sonship relation to God is the inward witness of the Holy Spirit. This witness of our filial relationship to God is seen most clearly in Christian

---

8. "Adoption" (v. 15) is the Greek *huiothesios*, "legally adopted son" (W. F. Arndt and F. W. Gingrich, *Greek-English Lexicon*, s.v.). It is a term used only by Paul and not found in the OT (LXX) or in classical writers, but the papyri manuscripts use it (James H. Moulton and George Milligan, *Vocabulary of the Greek New Testament*, p. 648; and G. Adolf Deissmann, *Bible Studies* [Edinburgh: T & T Clark, 1901], p. 239).

praying where we cry, "Abba! Father!" The expression, "Abba!
Father!" combines the untranslated Aramaic word *abba,* which
means "my father" in a very personal, intimate sense (Mk 14:36
with Mt 26:42) with the Greek word for father, *pater.* Only Jesus
uses this intimate form of prayer in the gospels due to His unique
Sonship (Mk 14:36). When Christians cry out to God, the Spirit
of sonship incites them to say as a child would to his father,
"Abba," or "my daddy."[9]

Furthermore, "the Spirit Himself bears witness with our spirit
that we are children of God" (v. 16). This is an additional witness of our sonship borne directly to our spirit. This consciousness
perhaps consists in the undefinable but real conviction through
the promises of God that we now belong to God (1 Jn 5:6, 9-12).
Note that the Holy Spirit is personal and that He is a distinct
being separate from man's own spirit.[10]

As children of God we are "heirs" of God. In fact, the only
way we get in on the future inheritance is as "fellow-heirs with
Christ" (v. 17).[11] Christ's inheritance is fabulous: "appointed
heir of all things" (Heb 1:2). Before Paul goes on to speak further
of this future glory which is like an inheritance that we receive
solely because of our relationship to someone else, he first mentions a condition for sharing Christ's glory: "if indeed we suffer
with Him" (v. 17). Here we discover a further implication of our
union with Christ (6:8). As Christ suffered before He entered
glory (1 Pe 1:11; Heb 2:9-10), so those who are identified with
Him also suffer before they enter the future glory. "In the world
you have tribulation, but take courage; I have overcome the
world" (Jn 16:33). Yet this is a suffering "with Him" since Christ

9. For some reason certain Aramaic words in the Christian tradition were
left untranslated into Greek: "Abba" (Mk 14:36; Ro 8:15; Gal 4:6); e.g.,
"*Eli Eli lama sabachthani*" (Mt 27:46); "*maranatha*" (1 Co 16:22). Perhaps
the precise shade of emotion in the original word or the traditional association was considered too precious to lose through translation. *Abba* was almost
never used in prayer by the Jews but was common as a child's address to his
own father (TDNT).
10. This point needs to be emphasized especially with the current post-
Christian age emphasis on oriental religions where no distinction is made
between God's Spirit and the spirit present in all the world.
11. This right of equally shared inheritance even to adopted sons is based
not on Jewish law but Roman (E. H. Gifford, "Romans" in *The Bible Commentary:* New Testament, 3:154).

is so united to His body, the church, that when the members suffer
for the gospel and for righteousness' sake, He as the Head, also
suffers (Ac 9:4; Phil 1:29; Col 1:24; 1 Pe 4:13). Why the suffering of the members of Christ's body must continue, Paul does
not reveal (nor does any biblical writer). There is a mystery connected with suffering that God has not been pleased to explain to
His creatures in the present. It is sufficient for faith to trust implicitly in God Himself who will ultimately reveal that suffering
was in some manner indispensable to the full manifestation of
His glory.

In the meantime, Paul shows that there are good reasons for
abiding faithful to God even in the midst of sufferings and perse-
cutions (vv. 18-30). Each reason is related to a special ministry of
the Holy Spirit. First the Spirit helps by creating a consciousness
by his presence of the reality of the greatness of the future glory
(vv. 18-25). Second, the Spirit definitely helps us to overcome
our natural weaknesses (vv. 26-27). Third is the assurance that
all things are working together for our good in the eternal purpose
of God (vv. 28-30).

First, in verses 18-25 Paul looks for encouragement to the Christian hope of the greatness of the future glory: "The sufferings . . .
are not worthy to be compared with the glory that is to be revealed to us" (v. 18). Just as real to us as our sufferings are now
is the certainty of our sharing the future glory of Christ (2 Co
4:16-18). To what does the "glory" that lies in the future refer?
First, it involves the release from decay and death of all of the
children of God. Second, there follows the release of the whole
creation from the captivity of corruption, sin, and death (vv. 19,
21, 23). This freeing from decay not only affects our individual
bodies (v. 23), but extends cosmically to the whole created order:
"the creation itself also will be set free from its slavery to corruption" (v. 21). Paul brings in the creation to show how great the
effect will be of the future revealing of the children of God.[12] So

_____

12. The word "creature" in the KJV in this passage is exactly the same
word which is translated in verse 22 as "creation" (Gk. *ktisis*). The latter
translation fits the other verses more suitably than the English "creature"
which restricts the thought to animate life.

great is this glory that the whole creation is anxiously longing[13] "on tiptoe," (Phillips) eagerly awaiting the revelation in resurrection bodies of the children of God (vv. 19, 23). Why is creation so expectant? Because nature has been so subjected by God Himself to futility that it too might share the same hope of release from decay that will one day come to God's children (vv. 20-21). The hope of man does not lie in cryonics (freezing the dead) but in resurrection.

Paul speaks of the present creation as (1) subject to futility, (2) not of its own will, and (3) subjected in hope. "Futility" (Gk. *mataioteti*) means "to no purpose" or "against the norm, unexpected." It may be Paul's commentary on Ecclesiastes 1:2, " 'Vanity of vanities,' says the Preacher. '. . . All is vanity.'" Nature seems to be imbued with the seeds of futility, decay, and death ("slavery to corruption" v. 21). Creation does not now fulfill its intended goal, which was to be man's wonderful habitat. The forces of nature seem from time to time to work against themselves and man, and do not achieve their intended ends. When drought, floods, hurricanes, or disease destroy vegetation and life, then beauty fades, vitality decays, and joy turns to weeping. This frustration produces what might be called a symphony of nature played in a minor key but with the expectation of a glorious finale. God has Himself subjected the created universe to a form of captivity resulting in this seeming lack of purpose in order to create "hope" in the glorious future release of creation along with the children of God (v. 21).

Paul does not say why God so subjected the universe; it may be tied up with man's sin and the "curse" upon the ground (Gen 3:17; 5:29). He who originally put the creation under man's dominion has now put the creation under slavery to the effects of man's sin and will make it a partaker of man's blessing in the future. So perhaps the next time we see nature frustrate itself in the crabgrass that infests our lawns, or the blight that kills the crops, or the excessive rainfall that ruins the melons, or the killer

---

13. The Greek word for "anxious longing" is *apokaradokia* from *kara*, "head" and *dechomai*, "to stretch out," so "stretch out the head forward" in eager or anxious waiting (TDNT). Only Paul uses the word (Ro 8:19; Phil 1:20).

tornado, or perhaps even the dilemma of the population explosion, we will think of the eager expectation of creation as it looks in hope toward our future glorious freedom in resurrection and its own deliverance from frustration, suffering, weakness, and decay ( Mt 19:28; Ac 3:21, "restoration of all things").

It is important in our day to note how Paul connects man with nature. The fate of nature is bound up with the fate of man. Man cannot solve his ecological problem without at the same time attending to his own problem. Note carefully that man can only find a partial remedy to the problems of ecology (creation) until the ultimate problem of human existence in sinful flesh is remedied by the personal return of Jesus Christ and the creation of new bodies and a new environment ( Rev 20:6; 21:1-2 ). Hence freedom is the significant mark of glorification for both creation and the human body.

But the present experience is no mere bumpy hayride. "The whole creation groans and suffers the pains of childbirth together" ( v. 22) and we also "groan within ourselves, waiting eagerly for . . . the redemption of our body" (v. 23). Creation can do nothing but wait, groan (moan), and hope. Christians also do not escape this frustration in their spiritual conflicts. We too then must wait, groan, and hope, but Christians have something the creation lacks, namely, "the first fruits of the Spirit." Firstfruits are the pledge or first installment of the whole harvest which is to come ( Lev 23:10; Ro 11:16). The precise meaning of our present trials and apparently meaningless sufferings is not clear, but because of the Spirit's encouragement we can wait to see the glorious outcome. Think of a caterpillar slowly advancing over the weavings of a tapestry. It can see only occasional changes in the color and sizes of the threads, but they would have no apparent meaning even if it could understand. Yet when the caterpillar emerges from its cocoon into a butterfly which can fly above the tapestry and see the beautiful design of the whole, the experiences he had walking over the weavings will be transformed.

Christians are not yet fully redeemed, even though they are fully accepted by God. They possess now a body of death (7:24; 8:10), but they also have received the indwelling Spirit who provides both enablement to rise above the Adamic natural life (lived by control of the sinful flesh) and a guarantee that our bodies will one day be freed through resurrection from death and decay (8:11; 2 Co 5:4). We are real sons of God now and adopted (8:15), but we are not fully the sons of God (adoption, v. 23) until our physical bodies also have been released ("redeemed") from death and decay (including sickness). The Spirit's presence in us is our encouraging guarantee of the greater things to come (2 Co 1:22; 5:5; Gen 24:53)!

In verses 24-25 Paul again poses a paradox. We were really saved in the past moment when by faith Christ became our righteousness, but we were not fully saved because we were saved "in hope" of the future complete restoration. Our present salvation includes the hope of the future resurrection of our bodies (Phil 3:21), but inasmuch as it is not yet realized ("seen") we must wait for it patiently (v. 25; 5:3-5). Faith is the means whereby we are given a salvation which includes hope. Therefore, faith and hope while distinguishable are inseparable in Christian experience. "Hope nourishes and sustains faith," remarked Calvin. Power for living in the present sufferings with Christ lies in the direction of this hope in our future glorification with Christ.[14] Truly the God of the future is greater than the God of the past (from our perspective).

Now the Spirit not only creates hope in us but also provides help for our infirmities (vv. 26-27). The tension between the suffering of the present time and the expectation of future glory certainly marks the Christian life on this earth and calls forth its groaning and longing. If the sufferings of Christ, which include all the forms of frustration and suffering under which we must live in the present age, weigh us down, so also does our "weakness" (v. 26). "In the same way the Spirit also helps our weakness" (v. 26) is Paul's description of the second help we receive in present sufferings. "In the same way" may refer to a comparison between the way the Spirit enables us in present suffering to experience the firstfruits of the certain and blessed future glory and thus wait patiently (vv. 18-25), and in the same way also the

14. On the whole matter of glorification, one should not overlook the excellent book by Bernard Ramm, *Them He Glorified* (Grand Rapids: Eerdmans, 1963).

Spirit relieves our weaknesses by His help.[15] Our main weakness is spiritual, that is, our struggle to allow the new life of the Spirit to have freedom in us as we live in a body corroded with sin and in an environment scented with death.

The English word *helps* translates the Greek compound word *synantilambanō*. The root word means "to take hold" (*lambanō*). The first prefix of the compound (*anti*) means "over against" or "face to face" while the second prefix (*syn*) means "together with." The great Greek scholar, A. T. Robertson, suggests the combined meaning to be: "The Holy Spirit lays hold of our weaknesses along with (*syn*) us and carries His part of the burden facing us (*anti*) as if two men were carrying a log, one at each end."[16] The word is found elsewhere in the New Testament only of Martha's plea to Jesus to tell Mary to get into the kitchen and help her (Lk 10:40).

Probably the most comprehensive example of how the Spirit lends a hand to help us in our weakness is in the matter of prayer: "How to pray as we should" (v. 26). Our problem is not ignorance of the *form* of prayer (how), but our weakness is an inability to articulate the *content* (what), that is, what we should ask for especially in sufferings that will meet our needs and at the same time fulfill God's will. The Spirit lends a hand by "interceding" for us to God (vv. 26, 27). Christians have two divine intercessors before God. Christ intercedes for them in the court of heaven in respect to their sins (Ro 8:34, Heb 7:25; 1 Jn 2:1). On the other hand, the Spirit intercedes in the theater of their hearts here on earth in respect to their weakness. The Spirit pleads to God for our real needs "with groanings too deep for words" (v. 26). Creation is groaning (v. 22); Christians are groaning (v. 23); so also God the Holy Spirit groans. As God the Father "searches the hearts" of His children—sobering but also comforting—He finds in their consciousness unspoken and inexpressible sighings. Though inexpressible they are not unintelligible to the understanding of the Father. Furthermore, these sighings in our heart turn out to

15. It is possible to understand the "likewise" as referring to *our* waiting patiently; likewise the Spirit on God's part helps our weaknesses (Gifford, 3:157).

16. A. T. Robertson, *A Grammar of the Greek New Testament in the Light of Historical Research* (Nashville: Broadman, 1947), p. 593.

be spiritual desires in the will of God because in reality they are the expressions of the Spirit's intercession on behalf of our weaknesses (v. 27). In this manner we can understand how God does "exceeding abundantly beyond all that we ask or think" (Eph 3:20).

When one of our preschoolers desires to write to Granny, my wife gives her a sheet of paper and a pencil, and she expresses her feelings in lines, circles, and zigzag marks. They are truly unintelligible signs. When Mother gets the paper back, she adds certain intelligible words to appropriate marks on the paper such as, "Hello, Granny" with an arrow to the first few scribblings, "We miss you" connected to other marks, and finally, "Come visit us soon. I love you, Lynn." Mother truly has interceded for Lynn to Granny, even as the Spirit intercedes for us to the Father.

Finally, verses 28-30 give us the third reason for patiently enduring suffering. It is the firm conviction that under the hand of the Sovereign Lord of all creation, "God causes all things to work together for good to those who love God, to those who are called according to His purpose" (v. 28). God has a plan. Everything in our lives contributes to the realization of that purpose. It is an all-comprehensive plan in that "all" things are included; not one detail of our lives is excluded. It is a cooperative plan in that all things are "working together" in concert; the individual ingredients, as in a kitchen recipe, have no virtue or ultimate significance in themselves apart from the providential combination into the divine pattern. The plan is beneficent in that the goal is "the good." It is also selective in that it applies only to those "who love God" who are in fact those "called" by God into His glorious purpose through the redemption effected through Jesus Christ.[17] Our good, C.S. Lewis points out, is to love God and fulfill His will for our lives.[18]

In verses 29-30 Paul focuses on the main events leading to God's eternal "purpose" for the Christian of ultimate glorification with Christ. He begins before time in the Father's foreknowledge and

17. A textual variant here in some ancient Greek manuscripts reads, "God causes all things to work." While it is possible this is what Paul wrote, the evidence and context strongly support the KJV rendering at this point: "All things work together for good" (Murray, 2:314).

18. C. S. Lewis, *Problem of Pain* (London: Collins, 1940), p. 41.

concludes beyond time in glorification; between these two, within time, comes calling and justification. Please note two prominent features of this plan. First, God Himself is the designer and executioner of each link in the chain. *He* foreknows and *He* predestinates; *He* calls and *He* justifies and *He* glorifies. Man has no active part in the design or execution of the purpose. Man's only part is his response of continual love to God (v. 28).

Secondly, all who begin in this plan by loving God also finish. Those "whom" He foreknew are those "whom" He called; "whom" He called He also justified, and "whom" He justified He also glorified. God starts with one hundred sheep and arrives in glory with one hundred, not ninety-nine. When contemplating the suffering and setbacks of this present life, nothing can be more assuring than to know that the present is only a small segment between justification and glorification in a total plan that has had three stages already fulfilled. It fills us with a sense of humility and worth and dignity beyond all comprehension and a sense of God's ability to meet every challenge that would thwart His purpose in our lives.

The "foreknowledge" (Gk. *proginōskō*) of God refers to more than mere knowledge beforehand (1 Pe 1:2, 20). It emphasizes the fact that salvation was initiated by God in His eternal loving choice whereby He chose us in Christ to be the objects of His loving purpose (see Amos 3:2; Eph 1:4-6). As difficult as it may seem, foreknowledge always depends on God's election or choice and never on our election of God (2 Th 2:13, 14). Those persons whom God chose to set His love upon are the very ones He also determined to "be conformed to the image of His Son" (v. 29). Predestination (Gk. *proorizō*) is almost the equivalent of foreknowledge (v. 30, only predestined is repeated in the chain) but emphasizes the goal or end in view while foreknowledge focuses on the persons involved (Ac 4:28; 1 Co 2:7; Eph 1:5, 11). The goal of God's electing purpose is that Christ might be the eldest (firstborn) of many brothers in glory who bear His very image or likeness (Col 1:18; 1 Co 15:49; Phil 3:21; Heb 2:10; 1 Jn 3:2). Glorification involves receiving the full humanity of Jesus in a redeemed body adapted to full expression of the Spirit.

Those who were predestined before time to this glory were

called and justified by God in time (v. 30). Calling refers to God's gracious direct appeal to our hearts to respond in faith to His free offer of pardon and new life in the gospel of Christ (2 Th 2:14). It too is a word associated with God's election (Is 41:9; 1 Co 1:26, 27); God calls (elects) us out of sin and death by the gospel of Christ. Calling is God's application in time of His election before time (Eph 1:4, 5). Our act of faith in the gospel of Christ secured our actual justification (acquittal and life) which has been Paul's burden throughout the letter. The final link that completes God's plan is our glorification with Christ (v. 30).

All the relative pronouns ("whom") in these verses go back to the first substantive phrase in verse 28, "to those who love God." Paul puts this first because he does not want anyone to miss it. Are these called because they love God, or do they love God because they are called? Theologians have debated this issue for centuries. The point that is important here in Romans is that Paul does not get caught up in this kind of theological speculation. All he says is that those who are foreknown, predestined, called, justified, and glorified are those whose earthly life since their conversion has been one great process of loving God.

Present distresses or reversals can never then be viewed as destructive forces against the Christian. Each fits into the present link in God's unfolding purpose. In some manner they are preparing us for the future revelation of His glory in the redeemed and in the whole creation. Reversals and distresses may pull us down. Yet on the other hand the contemplation of the reality of the future salvation (vv. 18-25), together with both the help of the Holy Spirit in our weakness (vv. 26-27) and the firm knowledge that all our experiences are working for our good in God's eternal plan (vv. 28-30) all combine to cause our spirits to rise in triumphant praise to God. It is He who has put us into an eternal relationship to Himself and freed us from all accusation (vv. 31-34) and all possibility of separation from His love in Christ Jesus (vv. 35-39).

Verses 31-39 conclude with the highest rung in the ladder of comfort which, from verse 18 onward, writer, like reader, has been mounting. Paul wants to apply this knowledge of certainty and se-

curity to the believer to elicit from the believer a feeling of con-
fident assurance. God is for us (in forgiveness and acceptance in
Christ). Who can legitimately accuse us before Him, for is He
not the very One who, to show His love for us, sacrificed the
greatest gift He could, His very own Son (vv. 31-32)? In the
phrase, "He who did not spare His own Son," we can see an allusion to Abraham's offering up his only son, Isaac, whereby he
showed his intense love for God (Gen 22). In the present instance God Himself is seen as expressing His supreme love for
us in not even sparing His own Son from death. If God has already so proved His love to us (5:8), how can anything that happens to us be considered less than the evidence of the outworking of His good (v. 28)? Dwight L. Moody once illustrated this
concept by remarking that if his friend, Mr. Tiffany, had offered
him as a gift a large, beautiful diamond, he would not hesitate
to ask Mr. Tiffany for some brown paper to wrap up the diamond.

Who can accuse us if God, who is the highest court of appeals,
has already acquitted us (v. 33)? Who can condemn us to suffer
the penalty and burden of a broken law if Christ Himself, the
Judge of man (Jn 5:22), has died and risen and is interceding for
us to God (Ro 8:34; Lk 22:31-32; Heb 7:24-25)? Grace and grace
alone has brought us into this certainty of acceptance with God.

If no person can accuse us, who or what then can separate us
from the eternal love of Christ for us? "Shall tribulation, or dis-
tress, or persecution, or famine, or nakedness, or peril, or sword?"
(v. 35). Paul has already experienced all of these except the last
and has found that his faith and hope were not destroyed but
enlarged (5:3-5). As far as the "sword" (death) is concerned,
Paul could refer to the Old Testament (Ps 44:22) history of the
persecution of God's people not as something marking God's dis-
favor but rather as (1) received for Him, " for thy sake," (2) continually, "all day long," and (3) delivered unto death, "as sheep
to be slaughtered" (v. 36).

Can any or all of these things in any amount ever detach us
from the love of Christ? *No!* Paul answers, because in fact it is
"*in* all these things" that God works out His plan for good (v. 28)
and causes us to overwhelmingly conquer through Him who

loved us" (v. 37).[19] No earthly affliction or infliction can disturb this confidence in God's love for us.

But further, Paul is also convinced that no factor of human existence (life or death), nor unseen spiritual power (angels, principalities), nor the expanse of space (height, depth) nor the course of time (present, to come), nor anything in the whole universe of God (any other created thing) can cut us off from this unbelievable love of God, the Father, manifested at the cross and poured out in our hearts when we received the grace of God (vv. 38, 39; 5:5). Yet in all this glorious victory we are reminded to not forget the means or the focus of such triumph since it is "through Him who loved us" (i.e., Jesus Christ) and "in Christ Jesus our Lord" (vv. 37, 39). An early fifth-century Christian witness well illustrates Paul's jubilation:

> When Chrysostom was brought before the Roman Emperor, the Emperor threatened him with banishment if he remained a Christian. Chrysostom replied, "Thou canst not banish me for this world is my father's house." "But I will slay thee," said the Emperor. "Nay, thou canst not," said the noble champion of the faith, "for my life is hid with Christ in God." "I will take away thy treasures." "Nay, but thou canst not for my treasure is in heaven and my heart is there." "But I will drive thee away from man and thou shalt have no friend left." "Nay thou canst not, for I have a friend in heaven from whom thou canst not separate me. I defy thee; for there is nothing that thou canst do to hurt me."[20]

19. "More than conquerors" is the Geneva Bible rendering (1557) of the Greek *hypernikaō* which Paul has used to express the superlative (*hyper*) victory (*nikaō*) of the Christian over all of life's threatening evils. We "easily win the victory" or we "come off as super victors" might also capture the force of Paul's word. The word occurs only rarely in pre-Christian literature (Arndt and Gingrich, s.v.).

20. See Henry Hart Milman, *History of Christianity* (New York: Crowell, 1881), 4:144.

# 2

## *The Faithfulness of God*

SOME UNDERSTAND this section on the Jew to be parenthetical to
the main thought of the letter. We will argue that chapters 9-11
form an essential link in the whole argument of God's righteousness by faith and fulfill a necessary and climactic function to the
whole doctrinal section. The problem Paul encounters at this
point in his doctrine is two-fold. First, if in the universal preaching of the gospel of Christ the priority of the message went "to
the Jew first" (1:16), why then has the Jew so little share in this
salvation? Hasn't the history of Jewish unbelief in Paul's gospel
shown that it is basically incompatible with the Old Testament
revelation?

Second, what has happened to the specific divine promise of
blessing given to Abraham and his seed? If the majority of the
Jews are found to be rejected because they cannot accept this new
faith which Paul preaches, how can God remain faithful and fulfill His Word of promise to Abraham? Or stated differently, doesn't
the gospel as Paul preaches it nullify the whole Old Testament
privilege of Israel as a people, which even the apostle himself has
previously affirmed (3:1-2)?

Paul's answer to this seeming discrepancy between his message
of the gospel and Jewish unbelief lies in two broad directions. He
shows on the one hand that the Jew's unbelief is not due to God's
unfaithfulness but their own faithlessness. If they are rejected, it
is because they have first rejected God (chaps. 9-10).

But this does not exhaust the answer. Paul also describes the outworking of a divine "mystery" in Israel's unbelief. Through Israel's unbelief, God's mercy and compassion will see unparalleled manifestation (chap. 11). More specifically, the promise to Abraham was not intended to be fulfilled to all Abraham's descendants but to a chosen seed or believing remnant both of Jewish and Gentile stock (9:6–10:21). Yet even though the integrity of God to His promises is fulfilled in the remnant, God also has in mind the eventual restoration of the whole people of Israel through their faith in Christ and through them a tremendous blessing for the entire world (11:1-36).

PAUL'S SORROW OVER ISRAEL'S UNBELIEF

9:1-5

PAUL'S SORROW (9:1-3)

Paul seems to move from the peak of joy in the last chapter to the valley of sorrow in these opening verses. The great apostle to the Gentiles (11:13), who repeatedly has had to speak against the Jewish concept of justification by works held by his fellow countrymen, shows that he is not a feelingless renegade from his own people. Paul is continually and deeply grieved in his heart over the unbelief in Christ exhibited by his fellow Jews. Three times he appeals to the absolute sincerity of his feelings (v. 1). So intense was his sorrow over their failure to receive Jesus as Messiah that he wishes that he might even be "anathema" (accursed)[1] from Christ if it would mean their reconciliation to Christ (v. 3). While this was not possible, his genuine love for those who were his "kinsmen according to the flesh" (not brothers in Christ) prompted this agonizing expression for their spiritual welfare. Do those who stand opposed to the gospel in our day so grieve our hearts?

THE JEWISH PRIVILEGES (9:4-5)

Paul has already mentioned the "advantage" of the Jew in 3:1-2

---

1. The Greek word *anathema* corresponds to the OT *herem*, "devoted to destruction" and often translated "accursed" (see Jos 6:17; 7:1; 1 Co 12:3; 16:22; Gal 1:8, 9). Like Moses of old (Ex 32:31-32), Paul wished to lose his own salvation for the salvation of his fellow Jews.

(actually only one was mentioned: the oracles of God). Now he elaborates eight privileges of being a Jew, against which his sorrow is intensified. To whom more is given more is expected and the deeper the sorrow when failure results. The eight-fold advantage is (1) the "adoption" was Israel's calling to sonship with God as their Father in the exodus (Ex 4:22, Ho 11:1); (2) the "glory" was God's visible manifestation whether in cloud and pillar of fire (Ex 15:6, 11) or in the sanctuary (Ex 40:34-35); (3) the "covenants" were five-fold: Abrahamic (Gen 15), Mosaic (Ex 20), Palestinian (Deu 29), Davidic (2 Sa 7), and new (Jer 31); (4) the "giving of the law" was at Sinai (Ex 20); (5) the "temple service" was the divine worship associated with the tabernacle; (6) the "promises" usually associated with the covenants included the main feature of blessings through the coming of the Messiah; (7) the "fathers" refer to the godly patriarchs (11:28); (8) the "Christ," who came through the Jewish descent (v. 5).

The last part of verse 5 has been the subject of much debate because of the way it may be punctuated (the Greek has no punctuation). One punctuation makes the expression a final doxology to God the Father: "May God, who rules over all, be for ever praised" (TEV). This is highly unlikely because a doxology at this point (that Christ came from unbelieving Jewish descent) would be totally inappropriate.[2]

The other punctuation refers the "who" to Christ but differs on whether "God" should be referred to Christ which precedes or to "blessed" which follows: "who (Christ) is over all, God blessed for ever" (ASV, NASB); or "Christ Who is God over all, blessed for ever" (Phillips). Either of the latter two renderings is preferable to the former because they refer Paul's doxology to the dual nature of Christ as being on the one hand Jewish flesh but on the other hand "over all" in His nature as Lord.[3]

---

2. E. H. Gifford, "Romans," in *The Bible Commentary: New Testament*, 3:169.

3. See John Murray, *The Epistle to the Romans*, vol. 2, Appendix A for an excellent discussion of the problem. Murray adopts the traditional KJV rendering as superior to others.

THE PROMISE, GOD'S ELECTION, AND ISRAEL'S PAST HISTORY

9:6-29

Paul has sharpened the problem of Jewish unbelief in verses 1-5. If such privileges and promises were given to the Jews by God, how can they now be largely cut off from the blessings of the Messiah by unbelief? If God makes a promise, can't He keep it? What becomes of God's righteousness which the gospel proclaims if God's truthfulness and faithfulness have apparently failed in connection with God's Word to Israel? If God has reneged on His promises to Israel, how could the Christian be certain that He would not change His mind toward him? If the promises of God are revocable, then how can one have joyous confidence in God's eternal plan through Christ? Both the validity of the promises and by implication the character of God are at stake.

Paul gives four lines of argument to answer this challenge. The first concerns the nature of God's promises as being rooted in the free and righteous elective purpose of God in Israel's history (9:6-29). Paul will show from Israel's history that God's promise to Abraham was intended to be fulfilled only to those whom He sovereignly "called."

It is important at this point to get some background in first century Jewish views of election. Problems which for years have entrenched theologians in chapters 9 and 10 might have been avoided if this material had been considered more seriously. Furthermore, by being preoccupied with these theological debates, many have also missed the real point of chapter 11.

The Jewish argument is well summarized by Berkeley Mickelsen in his commentary on Romans in *The Wycliffe Bible Commentary*.[4] Paul's Jewish opponents would present this view: "We have circumcision as a sign (Gen 17:7-14) that we are God's elect people. Members of God's elect people will not perish. Therefore, we will not perish." Rabbinical evidence shows that this was the attitude of most Jews in Paul's day. Hermann L. Strack and Paul Billerbeck have prepared a *Commentary on the New Testament* in which they bring together parallels from the Tal-

4. Berkeley Mickelsen, "Romans," in *The Wycliffe Bible Commentary*, ed. C. F. Pfeiffer and E. F. Harrison (Chicago: Moody, 1962), pp. 1209-10.

mud and Midrashim that shed light on the New Testament.[5]  In
Volume IV, Part 2, they have devoted an entire excursus (#31)
to the subject of *Sheol, Gehenna* (place of punishment), and the
*heavenly garden of Eden* (paradise). The following translations
include names of tractates of the rabbinical writings from which
their ideas about these places are drawn.

> Rabbi Levi has said: In the future (on the other side—what the
> Greeks called the spirit world) Abraham sits at the entrance of
> Gehenna and he allows no circumcised ones from the Israelites
> to enter into it (i.e., Gehenna). [Midrash Rabba Genesis, 48
> (30[a], 49)].[6]

In this same context the question is asked: How about those who
sin excessively? The answer is: They are returned to a state of
uncircumcision as they enter Gehenna. The next translation deals
with the question of what happens after death to an Israelite.

> When an Israelite goes into his eternal house (=grave), an
> angel is sitting over the heavenly garden of Eden, who takes each
> son of Israel who is circumcised for the purpose of bringing him
> into the heavenly garden of Eden (paradise). [Midrash Tan-
> chum, Sade, waw, 145[a], 35].[7]

Again the question is raised: How about those Israelites who serve
idols? As above, the answer is: They will be returned to a state
of uncircumcision in Gehenna. Here is a translation that looks at
the Israelites as a group:

> All Israelites who are circumcised come into the heavenly garden
> of Eden (paradise). [Midrash Tanchuma, Sade, waw, 145[a],
> 32].[8]

It is clear from these quotations that most Jews believed and
taught that all circumcised Israelites who have died are in paradise and that there are no circumcised Israelites in Gehenna.

To the claim that the Lord could not reject his elect people,
Paul first of all replies by emphasizing God's freedom, righteous-

---

5. Hermann L. Strack and Paul Billerbeck, *Kommentar zum Neue Testa-
mentum aus Talmud und Midrach*, 4 vols (Munich: Beck, 1922-28).
6. Ibid., 4.2.1066.
7. Ibid.
8. Ibid., 4.2.1067.

ness, and sovereignty. God acts freely, acts in righteousness, and acts sovereignly because he is free, righteous, and sovereign in His own eternal being.

THE PROMISE AND ABRAHAM'S DESCENDANTS, ISAAC AND JACOB (9:6-13)

Has God not kept His Word to Israel? No, Paul asserts: "But it is not as though the word of God [the promises] has failed" (Gk. *ekpiptō*, "to be in vain," "to lose validity") and by implication God's own faithfulness (v. 6). The reason why Paul asserts that the promises to Israel have not really been empty is that the promise has always been linked to the purpose of God determined by election or calling (v. 11). From the very beginning onward in Israel's history God has been selective in the application of the promise. He says, "They are not all Israel [true spiritual seed] who are descended from Israel [physical lineage]" (v. 6). The promise is valid only to those for whom it was intended.

Paul, in verses 6-13, uses two cases in the beginning of Israel's history to demonstrate that when God gave the promise of blessing to Abraham and his descendants, He did not have *all* the descendants of Abraham in mind. In the first place God chose Isaac rather than Ishmael to continue the promise made to Abraham: "Through Isaac your descendants will be named" (Ro 9:7; Gen 21:12); and the Word said, "Sarah shall have a son" (Ro 9:9; Gen 18:10). In an argument parallel to that elaborated further in Galatians 3 and 4, Paul argues that the descendants of Ishmael through the bondwoman Hagar are of the flesh and not the heirs of the promise. His point is that God moved toward fulfilling the promise through selection as in the case of Abraham's children.

But were not Abraham's children (Isaac and Ishmael) born of different mothers? God probably chose Isaac, it might be suggested, because he was born of Abraham's full wife, Sarah. To show that God's election has no reference to merit derived from the status or relationship of the mothers, Paul shows the same principle operating in *one* mother, Rebecca, and the birth of her twins, Jacob and Esau. God's election has nothing to do with the merits of special lineage or of an individual's own works. It all depends on God's sovereign will. God selected Jacob ("the older will serve the younger," v. 12) to continue the lineage through whom the promise was to be fulfilled even though such recognition was contrary to the Near Eastern custom of the right of inheritance going to the firstborn (vv. 10-12).

In verse 13 Paul appeals to a passage in the prophets to further support the practice of God's selection, "Jacob I loved, but Esau I hated" (Ro 9:13; Mal 1:2, 3). Love and hate in this context do not have to do with God's personal emotional hatred or love but with the *choice* of the one over the other to continue the fulfillment of the promise.

My children play a game involving various colored marbles. They inform me that I am to be interested only in marbles of a certain color, and I am not to try and take the others of different colors. In words similar to Malachi's they say, "Daddy you *hate* blue (marbles), and you *love* red (marbles)." Thus I choose (love) the red marbles for my purposes and leave (hate) the blue ones alone for other purposes. God's purposes in salvation, however, are never carried out without respect to a man's response of belief or unbelief. Paul will get to this point later (vv. 30-33), but first he must answer two objections to his concept of election.

GOD'S SOVEREIGNTY AND GOD'S JUSTICE (9:14-29)

The most natural objection to Paul's teaching on God's sovereign election (if correctly understood) is that it seems to make God unfair since He chooses one and not the other (even before birth in Jacob's case) without any regard to their works. So an objector might say, "There is no injustice [unrighteousness] with God, is there?" (v. 14). Paul's answer is disappointing but instructive. He simply abhors the idea ("May it never be!") and shows that God does exercise His mercy in absolute freedom of choice. Paul assumes throughout that God is just and His actions of election are also consistent with His justice.

To support his view of God's justice in His free choices, the apostle turns for further evidence to the Words of God to Moses and Pharaoh (vv. 15-18). If anyone in Israel's history should have been chosen for his good works, it would be the great lawgiver, Moses, but it is to Moses that God says, "I will have mercy on whom I have mercy" (Ro 9:15; Ex 33:19). Not even Moses was shown God's mercy except on the basis of God's own choice to bless Moses (v. 17). All God's acts toward man are on the basis of His mercy; man deserves nothing, because he is in rebellion. If God comes to man in mercy, man's status and blessing before God cannot be due to man's willing or achieving. This is Paul's whole position on justification by faith (chaps. 1-8).

What about Pharaoh himself (Ex 4:16-21)? It was precisely because Pharaoh hardened his heart that Israel was oppressed, and God could show His power in the exodus and proclaim His name to all ages through the Passover celebration (v. 17). Upon whom He wills He shows mercy, and "He hardens whom He desires" (v. 18). The hardening of Pharaoh's heart which resulted from his unbelief (Ex 4:21; 7:3; 9:12) was designed to show God's mercy. God's sovereignty even extends to the callousing of men's hearts. But even this severe action was a means to the end of showing His mercy. Pharaoh first hardened his own heart following the first five plagues, then God hardened Pharaoh's heart in the last five plagues.[9]

In the diatribe fashion (see 2:1) Paul utters the actual words of another objection, "Why does He still find fault? For who resists His will?" (v. 19). The objection is discerning and devastating. If God sovereignly hardens men's hearts like Pharaoh's, how can He justly judge them as hardened sinners since no one can resist His sovereign will? It is the problem of human responsibility and God's justice. Again Paul's answer is even more disappointing in one sense than the former but perhaps also more instructive. He does not answer the charge but simply says in the strongest way that man's position as a creature does not qualify him to contradict the Creator (vv. 20, 21). Man must be silent! Just as a potter may fashion his clay as he pleases (Jer 18), so God has perfect liberty to make of humanity what He pleases. As the pottery cannot answer back challenging the design of the potter, so neither can man (Is 29:16).

But someone may object, man is not a pot and he *will* ask ques-

9. Carl F. Keil and Franz Delitzsch, *Commentaries on the Old Testament*, 13 vols. (Grand Rapids: Eerdmans, 1949), 1:453-57.

tions! But Paul's reply rejects this kind of question because it presupposes the centrality of *man* and to try to answer it would tend to lower God to human reasoning and attempt to justify God theoretically. Rather, Paul affirms the centrality of God and will not lower God's actions to fit man's reasoning. His response demands that first of all God be acknowledged as God (1:21). Ultimately, as the potter is responsible for the vessel he fashions, so God is, finally, responsible for what He does in history.

Verses 22-24 expand the thought of the potter having the absolute right to make vessels for whatever end he wishes either for aesthetic ends or for more common, menial ends ("honorable use . . . common use"). Paul further draws upon the potter analogy but begins to narrow down the sense to his immediate concern. God makes "vessels [instruments] of wrath prepared for destruction" (v. 22)[10] and "vessels [instruments] of mercy, which He prepared beforehand for glory" (v. 23). Verse 24 makes it plain that Paul has *persons* in mind: "Even us, whom he also called." Further, "calling" in the whole epistle refers to the individual call to salvation and justification (8:30). One cannot then, regardless of the difficulty, weaken at least the latter part of the chapter's emphasis on individual election and calling (regardless of the earlier portions) to that of mere national or corporate election. Paul's very point is to the opposite effect, that is, God has by grace selected a group out of the nation to whom He will manifest His mercy (forgiveness), and He has fitted others to receive His wrath (deservedly because of their unbelief, vv. 30-33).

But lest we charge God with arbitrary rigor, it should be noted that Paul's burden is to show that God's deliberate design in election was to show forth His mercy (v. 23). In order to do this, God exercised much longsuffering (patience) toward the vessels of wrath (Pharaoh and the unbelieving Jews and Gentiles, in Paul's day) by not immediately destroying them but giving them opportunity to repent before His final power and wrath is revealed (2:4-5).

10. The Greek verb is *katartizō* which means "to suit," "to fit," "to establish," "to foreordain" (TDNT). The verb interestingly is passive in voice, which may suggest Paul is softening the active role of God in thus making such a vessel (although ultimately God is responsible). In verse 23 the vessels of mercy are directly prepared (active voice) by God for glory.

Paul's main point seems to be that when unbelief and hardening arise as in the case of Pharaoh and the majority of Jewish people in Paul's day, God has a purpose in history (as well as for the individual). This purpose is first of all to reveal His wrath against rebellion and thereby proclaim to the world His power. Second, through unbelief God will cause His mercy to be brought upon those whom He calls. Ultimately, then, history is redemptive in its purpose. In glory and in wrath through election God is working out His purpose in history of manifesting His righteousness.

In verses 25-29 Paul appeals to the Old Testament prophecies for the principles which substantiate his claim by references to God's announcement to choose an elect company of both Jews and Gentiles to participate in His mercy. To show that God had in mind to "call" (to salvation) Gentiles, Paul quotes Hosea 2:23 and 1:10, which originally applied to apostate Jews as "not My people" and "not beloved," to the effect that God would call to Himself those who were not His people (by application, Gentiles) and make them "sons of the living God" (vv. 25-26).

Furthermore, Paul quotes Isaiah to show that the Old Testament predicted that God would "call" not the *whole* nation of Israel through His promise, but only a remnant would be saved (Ro 9:27-29; Is 1:9, 10, 22, 23; 11:11). Again in Isaiah's day God's wrath was poured out through the Assyrians on a disbelieving nation (v. 28), but God moved also in electing grace to preserve a remnant or seed (v. 29). So in all God's dealings with men the promise of blessing (forgiveness) relates to the chosen seed who are of faith; and if unbelief prevails, it does not thereby nullify the Word of God.

### ISRAEL'S FAILURE HER OWN FAULT
### 9.30—10:21

Paul has argued that Israel's unbelief cannot invalidate God's Word because God's promise is based on the principle of election. He now turns to the human side of Israel's failure, their own unbelief. If God has elected some in sovereign grace to fulfill His Word, He has not thereby invalidated human responsibility. His election is not unrelated to man's belief. Israel's stumbling was due to her own misguided effort in attempting to please God through law obedience rather than by faith. "Christ is the end of the law for righteousness to everyone who believes" (9:30–10:4).

Furthermore, this faith righteousness which Paul proclaims, unlike the law, is easily available to all who will hear its Word (10:5-13). Yet Israel has heard this universally preached Word of Christ and has turned from it in disobedience as the prophets foretold. They are therefore fully responsible for God's rejection of them (10:14-21).

THE CAUSE OF THE JEWS' FAILURE (9:30–10:4)

While the Jew has not lacked enthusiasm for God ("pursued righteousness," "zeal for God," 9:31; 10:2), his commendable sincerity has not helped him before God because it was selfishly misguided. The Jewish moralist, in attempting to attain acceptance before God by keeping the law, has, in fact, not attained this acceptance (righteousness) as did the believing Gentile. Why? Because, as Paul has already argued through the first part of the letter (chaps. 1-8), all men are sinners and cannot approach God on the basis of good works. A man can come to Him only in humble acceptance by faith of God's provision in Christ (vv. 30-32).[11] This "stone of stumbling" (i.e., Christ and faith righteousness; 1 Pe 2:6-8) was prepared by God and foretold by Isaiah, the prophet (Ro 9:33; Is 8:14; 28:16). If the image of running is still in Paul's mind, then the picture of a runner tripping over a hurdle and losing the race vividly captures his point (vv. 32, 33).

The misinformed zeal for God of his Jewish kinsmen intensifies the tragedy of their rejection. It is Paul's earnest desire that they may realize their error and turn to Christ for deliverance from their sin (10:1-2). Charles Erdman commented that there would be no lack of converts to the Christian faith if all who profess to follow Christ felt for the spiritual welfare of their fellow countrymen this deep concern expressed by Paul for his own people.[12]

---

11. The use of "law" of righteousness in verse 31 is similar to the use of law in 3:27; 7:21, 23; 8:2 and means principle or rule or order.
12. Charles Erdman, *The Epistle of Paul to the Romans*, p. 101.

The error of the moralist begins with his failure to judge himself correctly in view of his own moral and spiritual shortcomings. Supposing himself to be all right or as good as others, he develops a spirit of proud self-seeking, which is the root of sin. He ends up by boasting in his own moral achievements ( v. 3; 3:27 ). In seeking to establish before God his own righteousness, the moralist overlooks God's way of righteousness which comes through faith in Jesus Christ. It is an ironic tragedy—zeal for God, but rejection by God. These statements of Paul should forever settle the thesis that sincerity in place of truth suffices before God. Sincerity indeed may be indicative of a right attitude toward God, but not necessarily, as the present case reveals. Nor can ignorance be pleaded as an excuse before God because no man is totally ignorant of God's truth ( 1:19-20 ).

Christ is an "end" ( Gk. *telos,* goal, termination ) of the law to obtain justification to all who have faith ( v. 4 ). When one submits to Christ as God's means for justification, it puts an end to the attempted ( but futile ) seeking for justification through the moralistic approach of law.[13]

### THE RIGHTEOUSNESS OF FAITH ( 10:5-13 )

In these nine verses the righteousness which comes through law ( v. 5 ) is contrasted with the righteousness based on faith ( vv. 6-13 ). The latter is not only available ( vv. 5-8 ), and universal in its appeal ( vv. 11-13 ), but rests upon the historical fact of Jesus' death and resurrection ( vv. 9-10 ).

What about obedience to the law? Was not the keeping of the law the prerequisite for having life ( Lev 18:5; Lk 10:28 )? If God gave the law and commanded total obedience to it, can it be maintained that obedience to it would have no relevance? Paul seems to argue in verse 5 that Moses taught that the achievement of righteousness before God on the basis of obedience to the law was at least a theoretical possibility. However, Paul argued earlier in the letter that the law came in to increase the trespass ( 5:20 ).

---

13. "End" of law here should not be viewed as teaching either that the law was fulfilled in Christ or that the *aim* of the law was to be a pedagogue until Christ ( Gal 3:24 ), both of which are true. Rather, Christ is the end or *termination* of the law both in the sense of 7:6 as well as in the sense that the believer no longer seeks for justification in the law.

It may not be impossible to reconcile these two opposites if we remember that when a man attempts to keep all the law he discovers that he is powerless to do it and thus judged sinful by the same law through which he sought acceptance and life (Deu 27:26).

The Jews' (and all moralists') real mistake, according to Paul, is not that they do not take the law seriously but they fail to take it seriously enough. Moralists count on two illusions. They believe on the one hand that on the ledger of life certain good works in the credit column will in the long run cancel out many of the debit marks in the other column and ultimately put them in the black before God. On the other hand, they also hold to the false belief that whatever does not balance up will be overlooked by God's indulgence. But God does not keep any such credit books of good versus bad, because He has an entirely different way of balancing out the debit column. Righteousness comes only through faith in the Lord Jesus Christ.

In verses 6-8 Paul combines references to the Old Testament law (Deu 30:11-14) with statements about the gospel. It is clear that the words "do not say in your heart" (v. 6) are aimed at the attitude of unbelief in the gospel. What is not so clear is Paul's use of the phrases "who will ascend into heaven?" and "who will descend into the abyss?" which are borrowed from the Deuteronomy passage. Does Paul mean that the words which were originally applied to the law in the Old Testament have equal significance when applied to faith in Christ? Moses' warning in Deuteronomy is against the taunt of unbelief expressed when a man claims that the revelation of the law is too difficult (impossible) to fulfill because it is inaccessible (in heaven or beyond the sea). Likewise, Paul sees the danger of unbelief in the gospel as evidenced in a man demanding before he will trust Christ to actually have firsthand empirical proof of the incarnation ("bring Christ down") and the resurrection ("bring Christ up from the dead").

But faith operates on the basis of the *Word* of divine witness proclaimed in the message of Christ and therefore salvation-faith is immediately possible when one hears the gospel message. How important this truth is that connects the truthfulness of the historical facts of Jesus' death and resurrection with the preached Word of the gospel witness. This means that when I believe the gospel message by faith I do not need to actually witness or be able to infallibly verify those historical events to have their certainty and efficacy immediately applied to my life.

Verses 9-10 describe the two-fold content of this faith righteousness: namely, (1) "If you confess with your mouth Jesus as Lord" (the divine king from heaven); and (2) "believe in your heart that God raised Him from the dead." The kind of faith which grants forgiveness and acceptance before God consists basically in two articles. Along with acceptance of Jesus as Lord goes the second, God raised Him from the dead. The resurrection is a crucial fact because it marks out Jesus, the Lord from heaven, as absolutely distinct from any other lord. He is the one in whom alone the Father has accomplished his redeeming work for man (Heb 1:3).

No special point should be made in verse 10 over the dual use of "heart . . . righteousness" with "mouth . . . salvation." The biblical idea of the heart refers to the religious center or core of our life and should not be limited to only the affections or emotions. What the heart believes will be uttered by the lips. As Paul says elsewhere, "No man can call Jesus Lord, except by the Holy Spirit" (1 Co 12:3; Mt 12:34). To "confess" means to declare, avow, profess, proclaim. It seems evident that the "confession" is to be made out loud before men, with the mouth, not by some other action.

Along with an affirmation from Is 28:16 to the effect that one who trusts in the Lord will not be "disappointed" (or "disillusioned"—TDNT), Paul strikes the note of the universality of this faith salvation in verses 11-13. Everyone (Jew and Gentile) who calls upon the name of the Lord shall be saved (Joel 2:32). The Old Testament foretold of this universal salvation available to all who evidence their faith in the Lord. Calling upon His name is an act of worship.[14] But why, then, haven't the Jews believed? Why have they been rejected in favor of the Gentiles? Paul now turns to this problem.

14. Murray, 2:58.

THE FAILURE OF FAITH (10:14-21)

Perhaps ignorance of the gospel is the problem? In verses 14-15 Paul constructs a five-link chain to emphasize that ignorance is not the cause of the Jews' failure. Men will only call (for salvation) upon one in whom they believe. Faith must have a proclaimed conscious object, which requires a message and a messenger. Finally, a genuine messenger or an apostle who is commissioned by the Lord Himself must be "sent" (Gk. *apostalōsin*) (v. 15). This last link is confirmed by a reference to the Old Testament where God approvingly mentions the ministry of *sent ones* (apostles) to Israel for salvation purposes (Is 52:7).

Paul abruptly breaks the chain at this point and raises the issue of Israel's unbelief, "However, they did not all heed the glad tidings" (v. 16). The hearing of the message was only beneficial when it was received by faith (Heb 4:1-2). "Those beside the road" writes Luke, "are those who have heard; then the devil comes and takes away the word from their heart, so that they may not believe and be saved" (Lk 8:12). Even Isaiah confirms the truth Paul is stating by predicting that the message (report) concerning the Messiah would fail to be accepted (Is 53:1).

In verse 17 Paul summarizes ("so") his main point by affirming the connection between the message proclaimed by Christ's apostles and faith which calls upon the name of the Lord for salvation. Saving faith, then, arises in response to the message (Word preaching) about Christ (His lordship and resurrection, v. 9).[15] Faith has a perpetual relationship to the Word and cannot be separated from it any more than can the rays from the sun whence they proceed.

Now in verses 18-21 Paul speaks more pointedly to why Israel failed to respond to Jesus Christ. Perhaps they, in fact, did not have opportunity to hear the gospel of Christ? Paul answers quite emphatically to the contrary, "Indeed they have." The language of Psalm 19:4, which Paul uses to describe the universal satura-

---

15. The Greek here would permit the thought either of the Word about Christ (obj. gen.) in the sense of the apostles' preaching, or the word originated by Christ in the sense that the substance is His Word (subj. gen.). In either case the authority of the Word is emphasized. It is the very Word of Christ (Jn 3:34; 5:47; Eph 5:26; 1 Pe 1:25).

tion of t¹.e world with the gospel message, has raised an important question (v. 18).

Does the revelation of God in nature, to which the Psalm refers, carry with it the gospel message? In this case Paul would be saying that the Jews heard the gospel in the witness of nature. While this sense is possible, the context argues for a different meaning. Just as the revelation of God in nature is universal (Ps 19:4), and makes no distinctions between Jew and Gentile, so the historical revelation of God in the gospel of Jesus has gone forth with universality to all places and to all peoples. Israel indeed had heard the proclaimed message in the first century at least. They could not plead ignorance of Christ. The faithful obedience of our first century brethren in spreading the message of Christ to their known world regardless of the cost certainly should convict us.

Finally, the apostle discusses a further reason offered to explain why Israel failed to embrace Christ by asking, "Surely Israel did not know, did they?" (v. 19). The sense of the brief question is sharpened if we more accurately translate "know" by "understand." Perhaps the gospel preachers spoke unintelligibly and Israel misunderstood their message? Again the answer implied is no for both the law (Moses, v. 19) and then the prophets (Isaiah, vv. 20-21) declared that God was going to work significantly among the Gentiles ("not a nation;" "nation without understanding") and as a result the Jews would be "jealous" and "angry" (v. 19). Such strong emotional response could not but be the result of first of all a clear understanding of the universal character of the gospel message which puts Jew and Gentile on equal footing.

Furthermore, the Gentiles' response was immediate and grateful, from a people who were not even associated with the Lord (v. 20; Is 65:1). Yet, to Israel, God through the prophet declared (Is 65:2) that He had unceasingly stretched forth His hands in unwearied love only to have his pleading met with rebuffs (see also Mt 23:37-39). Surely there is a great mystery surrounding why man rebels against his Creator.

It seems clear from this chapter that the Jews' failure to respond to Christ's Word lies neither in their lack of knowledge nor in their failure to grasp the meaning of the message. Their rejection goes back to their own choice of unbelief and disobedience. It is not because God has withdrawn His love and promises to them.

ISRAEL'S FAILURE NEITHER TOTAL NOR FINAL
11:1-36

Since the Jews have rejected the gospel of Christ, does this mean that they have been entirely rejected by God for salvation? Has the plan of God in calling this nation of people been frustrated by their obstinacy? Who will now do what God intended Israel to do? Paul's answer is two-fold and very definite. First, God has not totally rejected the Jewish people from salvation. Paul is exhibit number one that God still has a believing remnant, though the majority are rejected because of their unbelief (11:1-10). Second, God is not through with this people as a whole nation, but He has planned a glorious revival among them sometime in the future (11:11-29). These two aspects of the Jews' present and future are both introduced by a separate question in verses 1 and 11.

JEWS' FAILURE NOT TOTAL (11:1-10)

Paul asks, with all that he has just said in mind (10:18-21), "God has not rejected His people, has He?" (v. 1). The form of the question in the Greek expects a negative answer, so he answers immediately with the strong negative, "May it never be!" (see 3:4). The principal reason for his confidence in God's favor toward Jewish people is that he himself comes from pure Jewish ancestry and yet believes in Jesus as the Messiah. The existence of Jewish Christians in the world proves that God has not rejected the total Jewish community.[16] "God has not rejected His people whom He foreknew" (v. 2) reflects the language of Psalm 94:14 (1 Sa 12:22). God remains ever faithful to His covenant prom-

---

16. "Jewish Christians" is a term used to describe a person of Jewish cultural and religious heritage who has come to believe in Jesus as the Messiah (the divine king of Israel). There is a more modern trend developing, especially in the state of Israel, for Jewish Christians to drop the name Christian and refer to themselves simply as Jews who believe that Jesus is the Messiah, the *Mesh*him. The term "Christian," we should remember, was not used of the followers of Jesus until many years after His death and resurrection and at first only by pagans in derision of the way believers in Christ lived (Ac 11:26). The important fact is not the name but whether you belong to and follow the Lord Jesus Christ. Jewish conversion presents a special case of Christian conversion and must be so recognized.

ise to Abraham (Gen 22:17-18) and has set His love ("foreknew," see 8:29) upon an elect Jewish remnant of those who believe, which constitute "His people" at the present time.

Paul turns in verses 2-5 to one of the many cases in the Old Testament where the nation in large measure had turned away from God's will, yet there were still those who followed him. It forms a parallel to the problem of unbelief in his own day. Elijah's circumstances in the revolt against God incited by Jezebel forced him to conclude that he alone of the whole nation was still a true follower of the Lord (1 Ki 19:10-14). Yet God's Word came to him and revealed that there were some seven thousand others whom God had "kept" for Himself who were still obedient to Him (v. 4). Paul identifies himself with Elijah in his aloneness and also in the mild but encouraging rebuke of the Lord, who reminded the prophet that there was a chosen remnant out of Israel that constituted the true Israel through whom God's covenant purposes would continue (9:6-8).

"In the same way then [as in Elijah's day], there has also come to be at the present time a remnant [of Jewish Christians] according to God's gracious choice" (v. 5). Since the remnant can only exist by God's choice, it must be by grace and not on the basis of man's works. Paul digresses briefly in verse 6 to emphasize his main argument that appeared earlier in the letter (3: 27–4:25). God deals with men only on the basis of His grace (hence, man's faith) and not their works. Grace and works are mutually exclusive principles in winning acceptance before God. If God's election is the basis of the remnant's existence, then it must be based on God's grace which precedes all human works, otherwise grace ceases to be grace, and works cease to be works. In other words, if we confuse such opposites as grace and works, words lose their meaning (Eph 2:8-9; Ro 9:11).

But what of the "rest" of the nation of Israel who were not the remnant? Paul says they were "hardened" (v. 7) in accordance with the Old Testament predictions in Moses' writing (Ro 11:8; Deu 29:4), and in David's statements (Ro 11:9-10; Ps 69:22). Hardening is a divine judgment arising out of unbelief (Ro 11:20; 9:17-18; Heb 3:12-13; Mt 13:14-15). Unbelief brings blindness, insensitivity, bondage ("bend their backs," v. 10), and social discord ("table become a snare," v. 9). One cannot refuse the divine grace without at the same time positively opposing God (Mk 9:40). Such opposition brings God's active judgment in the present life much in the same manner as the three-fold reference to divine judgment ("God gave them over") in chapter 1.

The expression in verse 7 to the effect that Israel did not obtain what it sought for can mean nothing less than that the majority of the people did not obtain righteousness or justification before God (9:30; 10:3). The elect remnant obtained the justification by faith, but the rest did not. Here is further evidence that although Paul has groups of people in mind in these chapters (9-11) he is also in certain places talking about the relationship to God in salvation of individuals who make up these groups.

Jews' Failure Not Final (11:11-32)

If the majority of the Jewish nation stumbled over the gospel, even though a remnant believed, does this mean that God is through with the people as a whole or as a nation? Paul's question in verse 11 is very important: "They did not stumble so as to fall, did they?" That the Jews have "stumbled" into unbelief and disobedience the apostle has already clearly stated (9:32). But what does he mean by the phrase, "so as to fall"?

Some understand the "fall" to refer to Israel's final rejection as a religious community in the sense that God has purposed ("so as") as a whole they should never recover. The negative reply, "May it never be!" would then deny that this was true. Furthermore, the latter part of the chapter (vv. 12, 25-27) would also support this idea that God is not finished with the nation as a spiritual community when it refers to the future salvation of "all Israel."

The chief problem with this view is that it does not do justice to the rest of verse 11: "But by their transgression [stumbling] salvation has come to the Gentiles, to make them [Israel] jealous." In this use of the words, "by their transgression" (Gk. *paraptōma*, trespass, sin, 5:15), the reference is clearly to their stumbling into sin and unbelief.

Another sense, then, for the word "fall" is preferred. Paul's real question is whether the Jews' stumbling into the sin of unbelief was purposed by God so that they might lose their covenant relationship involving not only a future redemptive purpose but also a present purpose. Paul answers in strong abhorrence to the effect that they have not fallen down completely and proceeds to state two present divine purposes in Israel's stumbling: (1) that the gospel of salvation might go to the Gentiles and (2) that as a result of Gentile blessings the Jews might be stirred to jealousy and desire to come to Christ (11, 14). Both purposes are merciful in their design. This much, then, is clear. The sin of the Jews is temporary, and while it lasts, serves a particular gracious divine purpose.

In the first instance the immediate result of the Jewish rejection of Christ was the historical turning of the apostles to the Gentiles (Ac 13:46; 18:6; 28:28). Thus even in her disobedience, Israel still fulfills her calling as a link beween the Christ and the nations. Second, as a result of the conversion of the Gentiles, the Jews will be stirred to jealousy over the working of God among those who were formerly not His people. Paul's own ministry to the Gentiles can be viewed as ultimately a means of reaching at least some of his fellow Jews with Christ's gospel by making them jealous (vv. 13-14).

In verses 12 and 15 Paul contrasts and compares the present effects of the Gentile conversion with the future effects of Israel's conversion:

|  | JEWS | GENTILES |
|---|---|---|
| PRESENT | "Transgression" (v. 11): "failure" (v. 12); "rejection" (v. 15). | "Riches for the world" (v. 12); "riches for the Gentiles" (v. 12); "reconciliation of the world" (v. 15). |
| FUTURE | "How much more their fulfillment" (v. 12); "their acceptance . . . life from the dead" (v. 15). | "Fulness of the Gentiles" (v. 25). |

Paul sees a glorious future for the people of Israel as a nation and through them a tremendous blessing for the whole world.

This latter truth is highlighted in verse 15 by the difficult expression "life from the dead." The phrase probably does not describe the resurrection from the dead (most commentators since Origen) or the revival of the nation of Israel. Rather, it should be understood as a figure to describe some future glorious vivified condition of the whole world which occurs as a result of Israel's conversion.[17] Whatever tremendous thing Paul has in mind, it can only be described as the difference between death and life (v. 25).

To develop his argument further that the nation of Israel will still enjoy a future restoration as the people of God, Paul selects two analogies in verse 16. The "first piece" or "firstfruit" of the dough was a small portion of the newly kneaded lump that was set aside and, after having been baked into a loaf, offered to the Lord (Num 15:19-21.)[18] The consecrated offering of a part of the dough to the Lord was to sanctify, or set apart for God's purpose (make "holy"), the whole mass of dough. But who are the firstfruits of Israel? Some refer them to the Jewish remnant of whom Paul has been speaking in the context (v. 5). In this view the few Jewish Christians, like Paul himself, would be the pledge that the whole nation would eventually be saved.[19]

Most commentators, however, prefer to understand the firstfruit to mean the ancient forefathers (patriarchs) of Israel (v. 28). Because the first Jewish people were holy, that is, the patriarchs such as Abraham, who were truly consecrated to God, the people which came from these godly forefathers of the covenant form a whole with these patriarchs. Even though temporary unbelief and rejection has overtaken the nation, the covenant people will yet appear in the future in their real character and purpose as God's people. The temporary and partial unbelief of even a number of generations of Israelites, Paul would argue, cannot annul the continuing holy purpose of God destined for this people as a whole.

In the second metaphor of the "root" and "branches" of a tree, Paul further stresses the same point (v. 16). The tree bears the

17. Murray, 2:83-84.
18. The Greek *aparchē* (firstfruit) occurs a number of times in the NT: Ro 8:23; 16:5; 1 Co 16:15; 15:20, 23; Ja 1:18; Rev 14:4.
19. C. K. Barrett, *The Epistle to the Romans*, p. 216; and F. J. Leenhardt, *Romans* (London: ET of CNT, 1961), p. 286.

same character as the root. If the root (Abraham, Isaac, etc.) is holy (belonging to God), so are the branches (whole nation springing from the root). It is in the character of Israel as a covenant people, whose origins are good, that Paul sees the hope for their future restoration as a whole nation. Just as the believing wife or husband sanctifies (makes holy) the whole covenant marriage union of a believer and unbeliever, so that the children are not considered illegitimate or rejected by God (1 Co 7:14), so the believing forefathers of the Jewish people sanctify the whole covenant posterity in the sense that they are destined to fulfil! God's purpose as a covenant nation.

Verses 17-24 continue the figure of the tree with its root and branches. In this section Paul is concerned to ward off some dangerous misconceptions about his teachings that might arise in the minds of the Gentile Christians to whom he is writing. Because the Jewish people are likened by Paul to branches from a holy root (v. 18), it might be argued that their present unbelief and rejection cancels out God's covenant with the patriarchs and denies any future for the Jews as the people of God. Paul, haven't they blown it by what they did to Christ? Didn't they get what they deserved because of their unbelief? Hasn't God now taken us Gentiles to be his new people in place of the ancient Jews? This raises the important question concerning what kind of attitude Christians should have toward nonbelieving Jews. A number of important facts must be considered, and each seriously, if we are to develop a correct attitude toward these ancient people and toward ourselves as Christians.

Paul first stresses the humble position of Gentile Christians. Extending the imagery of the tree (v. 16), Paul states that even though a portion (historically) of the Jewish people have stumbled into unbelief, their trespass has only resulted in the breaking away of some of the branches and not in the uprooting of the whole tree, for the root is holy. Christians should not, then, feel that God is finished with the Jewish people as a nation. They are, despite their temporary rejection, still God's covenant people.

There is a very common misconception among Christians today. Some have disregarded as visionary all predictions of a future national resurgence of Israel as a spiritual entity, and appropriate the promises made specifically to the nation of Israel in the Old Testament to themselves in some spiritual sense as the distinctively new people of God, the new Israel. This belief still persists even though the present political state of Israel (since 1948) is forcing some serious reconsiderations. Instead Paul sees one continuous covenant people of God under the figure of the "olive tree." The root, or stock, from which believing Jews and Gentiles all receive their spiritual strength and nourishment, is found in the patriarchs who bear the original promises of salvation in Christ (Gal 3:16). The branches are either individual believers or generations of believers who derive their life from the continuous covenant family of God to which they belong.

The branches are of two kinds: (1) the original branches are the Jewish people, some of which have been "broken off" because of their unbelief in God's promise (v. 20), and (2) the "wild olive" branches are Gentile believers that are grafted into the covenant family of God. Paul's use of "wild" olive tree (v. 17) and the reference to grafting "contrary to nature" (v. 24)[20] further stress the humble position of Gentile Christians who were not originally even part of the tree.

Paul warns the Gentiles as a group not to gloat over the fallen branches (unbelieving Jews). There are two reasons for this: (1) Gentile believers are enjoying the blessings of God because they have been made part of the covenant promises given to the patriarchs of Israel and not the other way around: "it is not you who supports the root, but the root supports you" (v. 18); and (2) the Gentiles stand in relationship to God because of faith. If they begin to exhibit pride in their position, God will remove them from the tree in the same manner He removed the proud, unbelieving Jews (vv. 19-22). Faith (absence of pride, 3:27-28) alone provides man his only hope, peace, and security. The proper attitude of man toward God is always reverent "fear" (v. 20).

These lessons are greatly needed today. What could be more unscriptural than for Christians to despise or discriminate against

20. Though the normal process of grafting involves placing a good, strong shoot on a weaker stem to transfer the strength of the better tree to the poorer, Paul's phrase "contrary to nature" recognizes this and shows that he was familiar with the normal horticultural process but wished to use this analogy to press home his point.

unbelieving Jews? Not only have Christians inherited the blessings which were brought into the world by Jews, but did not even
Jesus say, "Salvation is from the Jews" (Jn 4:22)?

Furthermore, Gentile Christians must not be skeptical about
the problem of continuing Jewish unbelief, since it is much more
natural for God to put the Jew back into his own inheritance than
it is for God to save the Gentiles (vv. 23-24). It must be remembered that Paul is talking about groups of people or generations
and not individuals as such.

Paul now turns more directly to the prediction of the future
Jewish revival in verses 25-27. He still wishes to further warn
Gentile Christians against congratulating themselves for being
wiser than the Jew, wiser, since they responded to the gospel
whereas the latter rejected it. It should never be forgotten by
Christians that Israel as a nation and as a spiritual entity has a
glorious future in the outworking of God's purpose in history.
Since there are several important terms in these verses and each
has its own problems, it may be well to discuss each briefly.

1. The *mystery.* "Mystery" is Paul's characteristic way of referring either to a past secret purpose of God which has now been
uncovered and made known to men (Ro 16:25; Col 1:26-27;
2 Th 2:7), or to a future purpose that is made known now for the
instruction and attitude of the believer (1 Co 15:51). The mystery is this: a partial (not total) hardening (not blinding) has
occurred in the present among the Jewish people because of
their unbelief (v. 7) and will continue until the fullness of the
Gentiles is brought about, and then all Israel will be saved. Paul
here speaks of the nation of Israel and not every last individual
in the nation. He says in effect that the nation's hardness to Christ
is "partial," not total; temporary, not permanent ("until").

2. The *fullness* of the Gentiles. What does "fulness" (v. 25)
mean? A number of views are possible. In verse 12 Paul refers
to the "fulfillment" (Greek is same in both) of Israel as the opposite of their diminishing (only a remnant is now saved). So the
fullness of the Gentiles could mean their "full number" in comparison to the small number who up to Paul's time were converted. The fullness might be reached whenever in any generation the final person filling up the total number is converted. But

in the light of what the same word ("fulfillment") means in verse 12—no longer a redeemed remnant but a converted mass—it seems better to understand "fulness of the Gentiles" to indicate some sort of sweeping revival in the future resulting in the conversion of most of the Gentiles just prior to the great harvest of the Jews.

Others attempt to relate the fullness of the Gentiles to fulfillment of the "times of the Gentiles" spoken of by our Lord in Luke 21:24. The sense would be, "a partial hardening has happened to Israel until the fullness of the times of the Gentiles has come." Israel's acceptance is preceded by the moment in which God put an end to Israel's oppression by the Gentile nations.[21] But "Gentiles" in Romans 9-11 almost always means Gentile Christians (9:24, 30; 11:12-13), and "times of the Gentiles" has an oppressive, unfavorable connotation, while "fulness of the Gentiles" like the "fulfillment of Israel" (v. 12) has the sense of a favorable divine blessing.

One further modification of the first view deserves mention. The fullness of the Gentiles might have reference to geographical fullness, that is, it would refer to the full complement of the Gentiles, or the Gentile nations as a whole.[22] This note of universality of the evangelization of the Gentile nations is sounded by Christ in the Olivet discourse when He says. "And this gospel of the kingdom shall be preached in the whole world for a witness unto all nations, and then the end shall come" (Mt 24:14). Again, the reference as in the first view, would be to some great evangelization effort of Christianity reaching all the Gentiles that will precede the conversion of Israel and in some way be related to that later event. It need not mean that every Gentile would be converted, but enough would be to refer to the whole ethnic group or entity. The main objection to this modification, as we understand it, is that "fulness" refers more definitely to conversion than to mere evangelization.

It seems preferable to us to adopt the first view while admitting there are still unresolved ambiguities.

3. *And thus.* It may appear that this little "and thus" (v. 26)

21. Hendrik Berkhof, *Christ the Meaning of History* (Atlanta: John Knox, 1966), p. 144.
22. Erdman, p. 127.

is not important, and to isolate it smacks of pedantry. But if we make the text read "then" or "after this," we will not totally distort the sense of Paul, but we may miss the deeper thought. The use of "and thus" stresses some *logical* (not temporal) connection between the fullness of the Gentiles and the salvation of all Israel. The "and thus" might refer to the manner of Israel's deliverance, that is, that Israel will be saved by means of the coming Redeemer, described in the following words, "The Deliverer will come from Zion" (v. 26). But probably it is better to see the term as referring back to the whole mystery explained in verse 25: the strange detour by which Israel's partial unbelief continues until God brings in the fullness of the Gentiles.[23] Whether the Gentile fullness will provoke Israel to emulation or some other means will be used is not clear.

4. *All Israel* to be saved. Finally, what is meant by "all Israel" (v. 26)? Some understand Paul to be referring to *spiritual* Israel composed of both believing Jews and believing Gentiles (Gal 6:16). This interpretation was held by a number of early and later church fathers (Theodorus; Augustine, in some texts; Luther and most of the reformers).[24] However, the context and exegetical factors strongly favor an alternate view.

Paul's entire usage of the word *Israel* in this section of the book (chapters 9-11), especially in chapter 11, and even the preceding verse, make it virtually certain that he is denoting the ethnic Israel or Jewish people which could not include Gentiles. This more limited use becomes clear by also noting the subject of the following phrases: "their fulfillment" (v. 12); "they do not continue in their unbelief, will be grafted in" (v. 23); "their disobedience . . . these also now have been disobedient . . . they also may now be shown mercy" (vv. 30-31); and, "all in disobedience, that He might show mercy to all" (v. 32).

"All" Israel, then, must refer to the forgiveness of the whole Jewish people or nation, the whole ethnic group in contrast to the saved remnant of Jews in Paul's day and ours. It is the whole people, rather than a small part, that will be converted to the Messiah (so teach Origen, Chrysostom, Ambrose, Augustine in

23. Berkhof, p. 146.
24. H. P. Liddon, *Romans*, p. 217.

*City of God,* and Jerome).[25] In other words, the "partial" hardness will be removed.

In verses 26 and 27 Paul appeals to the Old Testament to support his position that the nation will one day be saved. He quotes from Isaiah 29:20, 21 and 27:9 which refer to the day when the Messiah (the Deliverer) will remove all ungodliness from Jacob (Israel) and forgive the whole nation their sins. This fact supports Paul's contention that God will one day restore the whole nation in the blessings of the new covenant. It is not certain whether the reference in Isaiah to the Messiah's coming refers to His first coming and the still future implication to the nation of that coming, or whether Paul had in mind the second coming of Christ. Either will do justice to the context.

Further, the existing fact of Israel's present unbelief does not militate against Paul's view of the full salvation of the nation in the future because Israel has a unique paradoxical relationship to God: they are at the same time both "enemies" and "beloved" of God (vv. 28-29).

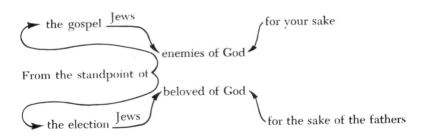

On the one hand they are enemies of God because they have rejected the gospel message which is of divine origin. But on the other hand, they are beloved of God because of His covenant-electing purposes for the nation. The latter phrase in each instance shows the eternal purpose in God's actions: "for your sake" explains why the majority of Jews are under God's wrath: it is

25. Ibid.; this view is also held by Murray; F. F. Bruce, *The Epistle of Paul to the Romans;* Erdman. For a strong case arguing the same view, see Peter Richardson, *Israel in the Apostolic Church* (New York: Columbia U., 1969), pp. 126-47. He denies Gal 6:16 refers to Gentiles.

because in God's providence the Gentiles were to be extended the call to salvation. "For the sake of the fathers" (the patriarchs, Abraham, Isaac, Jacob) explains why Israel will yet be blessed and received as a people. God's covenant promises to the patriarchs concerning their national blessing through salvation in the Messiah have not been abrogated despite the unbelief of many of the Jews. In verse 29, Paul emphatically states, "The gifts and the calling of God are irrevocable," that is, God's covenant promises are irrevocable because of His own faithfulness (3:3). This in no way overlooks the fact that individual Jews are either in or out of right relationship to God on the basis of their faith or that they are not accountable in judgment before God.

In verses 30-31 Paul reiterates the truth he has already stated several times. The salvation of the Gentiles was occasioned by the unbelief of Israel (v. 30). But Israel's salvation will be occasioned not by the Gentiles' return to unbelief but by means of the great mercy shown to these non-Jews (v. 31).

Finally, in verse 32, Paul concludes by drawing our attention to the relationship between man's disobedience and God's mercy. It is only in the context of disobedience that mercy can operate. Both Jew and Gentile are consigned to disobedience, but God's purpose is to show mercy. Paul is not teaching that all men individually will be saved but that God's mercy is extended to all people without discrimination (Gal 3:22).

## PAUL'S PRAISE (11:33-36)

Paul has been granted a small window into God's great plan for man. He stands back in awe and wonder. He worships Him by exclaiming, "Oh the depth of the riches both of the wisdom and knowledge of God! How unsearchable are His judgments and unfathomable His ways!" (v. 33). God's ways and thoughts are unfathomable to created intelligence. His exhaustless grace and goodness (riches), His providence (wisdom), and His understanding (knowledge) elude all attempts to trace out their causes or their directions because God is Himself the inscrutable origin of these characteristics (v. 34, from Is 40:13). Only poetry can do justice to this idea:

> Thy way was in the sea,
> And Thy paths in the mighty waters,
> And Thy footprints may not be known (Ps 77:19).

This is the reason for worship and the occasion for faith. This is ever God's ways with us: to reveal enough of Himself and His plans that we may glimpse the wisdom and movement of His ways and stand in awe, but only enough to reserve the mystery of His being just beyond the veil of our deepest gaze.

Furthermore, no one stands in relationship to God as a benefactor or innovator. God always acts in grace and love toward man; therefore, man can never build up a store of merit: "who has first given to Him [God] that it might be paid back to him [man] again?" (v. 35, from Job 41:11).

Paul closes with a burst of praise to the sovereign God: "For from Him [source] and through Him [agent] and to Him [goal] are all things" (v. 36). He is the center of all the created, historical, and personal order. God is the Alpha and the Omega (the A and the Z), the beginning and the end, the first and the last (Rev 4:11). If in this one case of His dealings with Israel, we can catch a glimpse of the vindication of His mysterious providence, in other cases we can wait for the explanation of His wisdom and the final evidence of His love and mercy. Surely, then, to *Him* alone belongs the glory forever and ever. So be it!

This is the expression of a faith which trusts when it cannot understand, which loves when it cannot explain, which reasons correctly that nothing but good can ultimately come from God to those who accept His grace through the Lord Jesus Christ.

### ADDITIONAL NOTE ON CHRISTIANITY AND CONTEMPORARY ISRAEL

This is not the place for an extended discussion of modern Israel in its prophetic, political, and religious aspect. But it seems hardly appropriate to write a modern commentary on these chapters and not say something about the relationship of Christianity to the newly formed political state of Israel.

### PEOPLE AND COUNTRY

We have seen by careful exegesis that Paul clearly teaches a revival among the Jewish people when they are restored as a pec ple to the blessings of God in the olive tree. The question is whether this future restoration must also involve the ancient land of Canaan, or Palestine.[26]

There is no doubt that in the Old Testament God's promise to Israel as a people is connected explicitly to one particular land area, Canaan (Gen 12:1; 13:12; 17:7-8; Deu 30:1-10). Dispersion and separation from the land is the repeated mark of God's judgment for Israel's disobedience, and the restoration to the land is the mark of God's grace to the nation (Deu 28:64-66; 30: 1-10; Is 62:4; Eze 36:8-12, 28, 33-36; Amos 9:11-15; Zec 8:1-23; 10:9-10). The latter two passages especially emphasize how closely the salvation of Israel as a people is connected to the land of Palestine.

But why Jerusalem and not Amman or Dacca or Rome? Could it be in part because Palestine forms the division between East and West? The Westerner looks at the Bible and senses its Eastern imagery and symbolism. While in the eyes of Easterners, the Bible is Western because its doctrine of creation secularizes the world. Israel is truly in the center (navel) of the earth (Eze 38:12). To a certain extent this mixing of Eastern and Western cultures has produced the current conflict in the Middle East between Westernized Jews and Easternized Arabs and Palestinians. There are also internal problems between the African-Asian Jews and the European-American Jews in Israel.

Yet the focus on Jerusalem (and Palestine) in God's plan must in large part be traced back to the Abrahamic and Davidic covenants as the outworking of the full realization of God's promises to them (Gen 12:1-3; 2 Sa 7:16).

Again, in the New Testament words of Jesus there seems to be further continuity with this same Old Testament thought. Jerusalem's destruction in A.D. 70 is not to be the last stroke in the connection of land and people, for Jesus predicts, "Jerusalem will be trampled under foot by the Gentiles until the times of the Gentiles be fulfilled" (Lk 21:24). This last of the great prophetic discourses reiterates with certainty that no matter how insurmountable the difficulties, land and people will one day be re-

26. I am here following the excellent summary of Berkhof, pp. 147ff. I do not think this author can by any standards be labeled "dispensationalist."

united, and Israel will fulfill its destiny in Palestine. Perhaps Scripture is not clear as to whether this return precedes their national repentance or follows it. It is clear that there is coming a time within this age, in which God's faithfulness will triumph over Israel's unbelief, and Israel will realize her destiny as a people, in Palestine, as the great evidence of God's saving activity in the world.

## THE POLITICAL STATE OF ISRAEL

The chief question for the Christian concerning the present state of Israel (established in 1948) is whether this has any connection with the predictions of Israel's national conversion and reunion with the land of Palestine. It is a difficult and complex question to answer, but one that is notably significant. When the Christian considers the way in which the State of Israel came into being, he may wonder if God could have had any direct hand in it.[27] If God is not directly involved in the formation of the present State of Israel, it would be difficult for Christians to maintain any special significance in it over any other temporary nationalism. Yet God has in Israel's past history overruled their questionable activities to accomplish in them His own purposes. Take the Jacob and the Joseph narratives as an example.

However, since I have no direct way of knowing which of these alternatives is actually the case, my position as a Christian toward the present state of Israel is somewhat ambivalent. Theologically, if I decide that God is preparing or actually beginning the process of Israel's restoration, I may be drawn in my sympathies to them and desire their welfare in the land. Yet I must also at the same time be repulsed from them morally whenever there is injustice toward the Arabs (especially Christian Arabs) or other peoples. Just because the Christian feels that Israel has a future in Palestine does not mean that he cannot be critical of any unethical and criminal acts committed by the Israelis.

The same attitude should hold true for the person who feels

27. George Giacumakis, Jr., "The Israeli-Arab Conflict in the Middle East" in *Protest and Politics*, ed. R. G. Clouse, R. D. Linder, and R. V. Pierard (Greenwood, S. C.: Attic Press, 1968), pp. 227-50; also "Christian Attitudes Toward Israel" in *The Cross and the Flag*, ed. Clouse, Linder, and Pierard (Carol Stream, Ill.: Creation House, 1972), pp. 203-15.

that the present state of Israel is not God's doing but merely man's. He cannot lightly dismiss or overlook acts of injustice done by Arabs or their leaders to their own people or to Israelis. In the present conflict the Christian must not identify totally with either the Arab or the Israeli political position. Both peoples have rights to the land historically. Instead he must be the reconciling ingredient between the two parties. Above all the Christian must treat all :nen as human beings, created in the image of God, worthy of respect and loving compassion.

THE MILLENNIAL KINGDOM

While there are numerous worthy Christian views on the question of a future divine earthly kingdom of peace established in history, it seems quite appropriate to think of this kingdom in association with the restoration of Israel as a people. The Old Testament views this kingdom of peace as occurring within history and centered in Israel (Is 2:2-4; 4:1-6; 9:6-7; Zec 14:8-11). Furthermore, in the one universally agreed upon clear passage in the New Testament (Rev 20:7-9) touching the question, a recovered Israel is seen as the center of the kingdom. The importance of discussing the whole modern utopian kingdom idea in the context of the biblical data on a restored Israel cannot be overestimated in the light of contemporary Marxist, Reichian,[28] or the Valhalla and all fools' paradise concepts.[29]

PROSPECTS OF WORLD REVIVAL

It has been shown exegetically that the interpretation of Paul's thought favors the view that there will be an extensive expansion of Gentile Christianity just prior to and in connection with the conversion of Israel. Are there signs that our era may be close to this? Of course, while any answer to this question must be speculative, there are several interesting facts to note. A noteworthy revival of large scope can be observed among American youth that appears to have prospects of growing to a worldwide movement and is already creating a "Jews for Jesus" movement

---

28. Charles Reich, *The Greening of America* (New York: Random, 1970), chap. 9, n. 3.
29. Berkhof, p. 153.

within its wake. As subjective as it may seem, there are numerous leaders in the evangelical church who feel we are on the brink and may be into a great worldwide revival.[30]

Finally, one is greatly impressed that in Israel today the Bible is the center of cultural focus. Each young person must memorize in Hebrew the entire historical books (Genesis through Chronicles) plus the prophets (Isaiah through Zechariah) before he can graduate from high school! While largely of historical and moral emphasis, this preparation of Jewish minds and hearts might in the future play a significant role in the nation's repentance to the Messiah. There is also a significant openness in Israel today toward discussing the relationship between Jews and Christians.

Thus Paul has dealt decisively with the major objection to his doctrine of God's faithfulness raised by Jewish unbelief: Israel has stumbled due to their own unfaithfulness, not God's, and furthermore God is working out in the Jewish people's unbelief a divine mystery which will magnify His mercy in an unparalleled manner (chaps. 9-11).

Paul's main argument of the book is now completed (1:18—11: 36). There yet remain several areas of more immediate concern pertaining to the outworking of this new life in Christ as it touches the real world of the Roman Christians.

30. Bill Bright, *Come Help Change the World* (Old Tappan, N.J.: Revell, 1970; Rufus Jones, "Will the Church Miss It?," *Bulletin of the Conservative Baptist Missions* (Fall 1971); Robert E. Coleman, "The Coming World Revival?," *Christianity Today* 15, no. 21 (July 16, 1971): 10-12; "The New Christians," *Christianity Today* 15: 20-23; "The New Rebel Cry: Jesus Is Coming!," *Time* 97, no. 25 (June 21, 1971): 56-63; "Jews for Jesus," *Time* 99, no. 24 (June 12, 1972): 66-67.

# 3

## *The Christian Way*

### 12:1—15:13

As IN ALL his other letters, Paul first sets forth the theological facts of Christianity and then follows out these truths into several concrete matters of actual Christian living in the world. In earlier chapters the apostle has already struck the note of moral renewal of the entire life. Such new life is inseparably wed to God's action of forgiveness (chaps. 6-8).

It should be carefully noted that Paul, unlike many preachers today, bases his call to Christian character upon Christian doctrine; he traces the expression of Christlikeness to belief. We will not find in Paul the often repeated but erroneous sharp distinction between "doctrine" and "life." Exhortations to live a certain type of ethical life which do not grow out of and find their basis in the gospel facts and redemptive message are mere moralisms, impotent to effect the real transformation of the moral life. To make any significant difference, then, between Paul's doctrinal sections and the practical sections manifests a failure to grasp this relationship. Furthermore, it should also be noted that the sections of doctrinal teaching embody ethical teaching and the sections of ethical teaching before us implicitly or explicitly teach doctrine.

But now the question could be put to Paul; just what, precisely, is the relationship between all this theology and doctrine and my actual Christian experience and conduct?

More specifically, Christian ethics is the application of Christian redemption or what is called sanctification. Our conduct springs from union with Christ (6:1-4). Jesus Himself constitutes for

67

us both the form and through the Spirit the actualizing or transforming power of the Christian life-style. Our motivation for
this life of discipleship lies in the desire to be obedient to Christ
which is an essential element in faith (1:5), and as an expression
of our deep gratitude to God who has shown to us His forgiving
and justifying mercy.

In the following chapters, Paul sketches the specific relevance
of the obedience of faith in Jesus Christ to the more general but
actual situations of life. Three major themes are touched upon:
(1) the relations of Christians to one another (12:3-13); (2) the
relations of Christians to non-Christian society (12:14—13:14);
and finally (3) a special problem in the relationship of believers
to one another, arising from their differences in cultural backgrounds (14:1—15:6). While the somewhat loose connection in
thoughts through the chapters emphasizes the spontaneity of
the Christian ethic as it confronts the complicated spectrum of
ethical situations, there is nevertheless an underlying regularity
in the application of the principle of life in the new being in
Christ, which is to walk in love.

### THE LIVING SACRIFICE
### 12:1-2

Paul begins with the foundation of all Christian living. In these
two verses we find the secret that unlocks the unlimited possibili-
ties of genuine Christian life in the world. Calling the Christians
in Rome brethren, the apostle appeals to them to make the supreme offering of complete dedication to God.

Paul bases his appeal on the "mercies of God" (v. 1). The best
clue to the meaning of this statement is found in the "therefore"
which indicates that Paul grounds his present appeal on what he
has previously said in his letter. God's mercy means God's merciful activity toward sinful man through Christ which Paul has
been expounding in the previous sections of the book and especially in chapters 9—11 (see 11:32). A Christian, then, is one
who has experienced the mercy of God.

But what are Christians to do? They are admonished, "Present
your bodies a living and holy sacrifice." The language draws upon
the sacrificial ritual of the Old Testament offerings: "present"

(offer on the altar), "sacrifice," "holy," "acceptable to God." Straining for some adequate image of the proper response of the believer to God's mercies, Paul, as previously (3:21), thinks of the sacrifices and especially the burnt offering (Lev 1:3-17). When an Israelite wanted to express his devotion to the Lord, he selected an appropriate animal or bird and brought it to the tabernacle to present it to the Lord. He laid his hands on the head of the animal, signifying substitutionary identification, and killed it, whereupon the priest burned the entire carcass upon the sacrificial altar. The offering was "holy" to the Lord in that it was wholly His (priest did not get any part). This act of worship and service was an "acceptable" odor to the Lord (Eph 5:2).

By "body" Paul does not mean our personalities or selves but our physical bodies with all their functions (6:6, 12; 8:10, 11, 23).[1] We are to serve God in these temporal earthen bodies, not in some imagined other-worldly vision or fancy. By stressing the sacrifice of the body Paul may have been countering certain latent Greek philosophical ideas which taught the deprecation of the body and man's eventual liberation from its captivity. Perhaps some thought that because the "body is dead because of sin" (8:10), it could not be acceptable to God for service.

"Spiritual service of worship" is more difficult. The word "service" (Gk. *latreia*) means to serve God by sacrifice. Since the whole cultic service of the priests in the Old Testament was viewed as a service before God, the same term has both the connotation of service to God and worship of God. Under the new covenant, in this age, every believer is a priest and can serve God by the sacrificial offering of his body in an act of worship to Him (1 Pe 2:9).

This service is further described as "spiritual" (Gk. *logikē*). While the Greek word Paul uses is related to the Greek for "reason" or "rational" (Eng., logical), the meaning may come closer to the thought of something that is true, or has inner reality in contrast to the merely external, material form. Worship in

---

1. Paul may not mean to exclude the self or person from his use of *body*, but there is no warrant to follow Bultmann and others here to see only the self. Man is a whole being from the biblical view, including the body as a prime ingredient.

both Judaism and pagan ritual tended toward the outward, more material form.[2] The Christian, in contrast to these external ritual religions, is to present his physical body as an act of true, inner, Spirit-directed service to God (Ro 1:9; Phil 3:3; Jn 4:23, 24).

The complete abandonment of our bodies to God's service constitutes the indispensable foundation or core of Christian living. Such a commitment should be made as a decisive, accomplished event, as the Greek tense of "present" suggests. All future decisions and actions will constantly be made in keeping with this initial step. Perhaps the best analogy is marriage. From the first act of each giving themselves totally to the other there follows a whole life lived together in the context of that original pledge.

We are simply kidding ourselves if we are trying to do Christian things and yet have never pledged ourselves fully to Jesus Christ. God's grace is free, but it is not cheap, for God gave us the most costly gift He could give, the suffering unto death for our sins of His own beloved Son. The discovery of this gift is like finding an incomparable pearl or a million-dollar treasure in our backyard (Mt 13:44-46). What lesser response to this love and mercy of God would be enough? As Isaac Watts has written,

> But drops of grief can ne'er repay
> The debt of love I owe;
> Here, Lord, I give myself away,
> 'Tis all that I can do.

As the late Sam Shoemaker has stated, to be a Christian means to give as much of myself as I can to as much of Jesus Christ as I know.

In verse 2 Paul describes the general nature of the growth process which is the natural and inseparable outworking of our supreme act of divine service related in verse 1. "This world" means this world which "is passing away" (1 Jn 2:17) and probably should be rendered as "age" (Gk. *aiōn*). The term *age* in biblical teaching views the present world as under the control of various alien powers such as sin, death, the flesh, covetousness (Gal 1:4). Its chief characteristic is lust or selfishness (1 Jn 2:

2. F. J. Leenhardt, *Romans*, p. 303, cites some examples of the word from Hellenistic Jewish texts where it denotes what is interior, what concerns the deepest being of man, in contrast to what is formal, external, or theatrical.

15-16). The world, or present age, has much more to do with attitudes and values than things; it is much more related to selfishness than certain kinds of activities. This age will pass away (1 Co 7:31); it has no permanence; it is only fashionable; it acts out a part and holds the stage, but it is without real being. Once a man realizes this, how foolish it is to join in with this "flick" which is projected on such a shaky screen. There is something better in Christ.

Paul warns his readers not to be "conformed" to this age. The word means to be poured into the mold of something and thereby to shape the outward appearance, to rubber stamp something. Phillip's translation has: "Don't let the world around you squeeze you into its own mould." Or in keeping with our previous thought it may be translated, "Stop letting this age give you your lines in its flick."

But Paul does not stop with the negative as do so many Christians. He goes on to admonish that they should allow the new age of the reign of God to break into their lives and "transform" (literally, metamorphose) them. Paul's word here is the same term found in the "transfiguration" of Jesus (Mt 17:2). He uses the word to describe the "changing" of believers into the image of Christ by the Holy Spirit as they reflect the glory of Christ (2 Co 3:18). This is no mere imitation of Christ but the outworking of the divine presence and power in the life. That the "mind" needs "renewal" shows how radically different Paul's idea of the mind is from Greek thought, which exalted the mind to almost divine status. The mind here, however, implies much more than man's intellectual activities but refers to the deepest springs of human existence and includes both man's willing and knowing faculties. Since the writing of Charles Reich's, *The Greening of America*, it may be more contemporary to call this "consciousness." It is a whole way of viewing the world and our experiences.[3]

The purpose or goal of this constant renewal of the mind is that you might "prove what the will of God is" (v. 2). To "prove" does not mean to test whether God's will is good or bad, but it

3. Charles Reich, *The Greening of America*, p. 14. Perhaps "Consciousness IV" would be appropriate to describe the changed world outlook of the truly renewed Christian mind; see Harry Blamires, *The Christian Mind* (London: SPCK, n.d.).

means to "try and approve" the will of God. In the consciousness of a person who is being transformed by Christ's Spirit, there lies the possibility of actually recognizing and doing the will of God in every human situation (Eph 5:9-10). In the testing and affirming of what is actually the will of God, the believer will also discover that it is precisely equivalent to the "good," to the "acceptable," and to the "perfect" in God's eyes in each situation. By following out these terms in Paul's usage a further clue can be obtained as to what precisely constitutes the will of God.

Here then in the first two verses is Paul's way of restating Jesus' call, "If any one wishes to come after Me, let him deny himself, and take up his cross, and follow Me. For whoever wishes to save his life shall lose it; but whoever loses his life for My sake shall find it" (Mt 16:24, 25). There will be found a constant tension in the Christian life between the present age in which we live and the age to come which has, in some measure, through the Holy Spirit already broken into our lives. There is a wrong way of staying in the world, just as there is a wrong way of fleeing from it.[4]

Christianity is change—radical, revolutionary change at the center of human consciousness. Paul's thought strikes devastatingly at every form of Christianity which is stagnant, complacent, proud of its accomplishments, or not radical enough to stand in judgment over every aspect of its relationship to the current age—whether political, social, personal or ecclesiastical.

### THE CHRISTIAN COMMUNITY

### 12:3-8

In the practical outworking of our deeply personal relationship to Christ, we will be confronted immediately with the fact that Christianity involves a people. One cannot be Christlike alone. Every Christian is united inseparably to all Christians in the one body in Christ (vv. 4, 5). Paul, in an epistle to the Corinthian believers, has already elaborated more fully on this thought (1 Co 12).

---

4. One good modern exposition of discipleship is Dietrich Bonhoeffer, *The Cost of Discipleship.* One does not have to agree with all of Bonhoeffer's theological conclusions to reap a rich profit from his understanding of obedience to God.

Furthermore, this section of Paul's letter illustrates the out-working of the first principle of Christian ethics stated in verse 2. Such may be the force of the word *for* at the beginning of the paragraph. One of the characteristics of this age which Christians are not to copy is pride (v. 2). Pride always has reference to others and must be seen as one of the prime roots of dissension. Paul may have had some knowledge of one group of Christians in Rome who thought they were better than others (11:18-21; 14:1-4). So he exhorts, "to every man among you not to think more highly of himself than he ought to think; but to think so as to have sound judgment, as God has allotted" (v. 3).

Humility, contrary to general opinion, is not assuming the least role, or taking the lowest notch on the totem pole. Rather, humility is an attitude and action which results from taking an honest look at where we best fit into the whole of God's work as He has determined by His gifts to us. Paul himself, for example, exercises his gift as an apostle by exhorting the Roman Christians prefacing his exhortations with the words, "Because of the grace that was given me" (15:15). Pride assumes or desires more prerogative than God has given to us. It is an exaggerated self-esteem. False humility, on the other hand, tends to assume a lesser role than the Lord has assigned. Therefore, each person is to "have sound judgment" or to hold a balanced viewpoint of his harmonious contribution to the whole body (vv. 4, 5).

The "measure of faith" (v. 3) certainly should be understood as the same as "gifts that differ according to the grace given to us" (v. 6) and corresponds to Paul's similar statements about gifts in 1 Corinthians 12 and Ephesians 4. Gifts of the Spirit are given to every believer. These spiritual enablements are differentiated and yet interlaced within the church so that there is a preservation of the beautiful relationship of the uniqueness of each individual contribution together with the importance and necessity of the community of the redeemed for the mutual edification and maturing of each individual person (Eph 4:13-16).

An individual Christian must not then think of himself as the whole church but as a petal to the flower. In realizing this truth I must constantly affirm two things: (1) I, or my group, do not have all the truth or all the gifts, and (2) the other person or

group may have truth and gifts I do not have. So to be whole
I must have fellowship and dialogue with all true Christians
worldwide. Paul enumerates seven such gifts in this passage.
The list should not be thought of as exhaustive or without special
significance in Paul's mind with respect to the Roman Christians'
needs and problems.[5] It is interesting to ask why no special
"charismatic" type gifts are mentioned as they are in the Corinthian correspondence (1 Co 12; 14).

Prophecy is mentioned first (v. 6). In the other lists of gifts
"apostle" takes preeminence even over a prophet (1 Co 12:28;
Eph 4:11). Since no apostle had apparently yet ministered to
the Roman Christians (15:20), Paul omits mention of it. The
prophetic gift in both the Old and New Testaments involves the
receiving of a message from God and communicating it to men.
Frequently, but not always, the prophet predicted future events
(Ac 21:10, 11) as well as giving the Word of God for the contemporary situation.

The church stands in need of this ministry today. Those who
can sensitively discern the movement of God in contemporary
events and are able to apply the biblical revelation dynamically to
our times may be modern day prophets such as Francis Schaeffer.[6]
Of course, their words are not infallible and must always be
evaluated critically in the light of Scripture (1 Co 14:29), especially by those who have the gift of "discerning of spirits" (1 Co
12:10).

The prophet is to use his gift "according to the proportion of his
faith." This expression might mean that the prophet must speak
in agreement with the faith, that is, scripture doctrine. However,
it is better in the context to understand the exhortation as a further subtle reminder by the apostle that the prophet is not in
pride to go beyond his appointed authority, but should exercise
his gift in exact agreement with the divine grace of enablement
which has been given to him. The same warning would hold

---

5. One should study more than a single tradition in the interpretation of
the gifts; e.g., John Walvoord, *The Holy Spirit* (Wheaton, Ill.: Van Kampen,
1954), chaps. 19, 20; and Donald Bloesch, *The Reform of the Church*
(Grand Rapids: Eerdmans, 1970), chap. 9, form a good comparison.
6. Francis A. Schaeffer, *Death in the City*.

true for the other gifts as well. Those who minister their gifts should be neither negligent nor pretentious.

The next gift mentioned is "service," or ministry (v. 7). This gift should not be thought of as one involving merely a call to be a preacher or missionary but means all forms of service, especially to the needy (Ro 15:25, 31; 2 Co 8:4). It may also refer to the deacon's work (Ac 6:1-3; 11:29; Phil 1:1; 1 Ti 3:8, 10, 12, 13). This gift and its ministry should not be regarded as less spiritual because it deals with material needs. A man or woman (Ro 16:1) may give full time to such services without coveting higher or allegedly more spiritual ministries (1 Ti 3:13).

"Teaching" (v. 7) involves more systematic explanation and application of Christian truth than mere preaching, such as Paul has given in this letter to the Romans (Ac 13:1; 15:35). While all prophetic preaching contains explanation (1 Co 14:2, 21) and all teaching should have contemporary application, the prophet is more concerned with proclaiming a direct Word from God to the immediate historical situation, whereas the teacher will explain and relate this Word to the rest of Scripture and its great themes. The effective ministry of the Word of God needs both gifts. If they are not found in one man, which is rare, then provision should be made for a dual ministry.

As for "exhortation" (v. 8), Paul may have reference either to the gift of ministering consolation (Gk. word is the same) to those in affliction or to the gift of exhorting men to arouse their spirits and encourage their hearts toward God and His will. Both aspects are related. Have you ever left the presence of some Christian, saying to yourself: Oh how thankful to God I am for that person's life; how glad I am to be a Christian! I believe this is the ministry of exhortation that we all need in a day of recurring waves of less than zealous Christianity.

The one who "gives" (or contributes) is to do it with "liberality," or better, with "unmixed motive of the heart" (2 Co 8:2; 9:11, 13; 11:3; Eph 6:5; Col 3:22). While it is possible to understand Paul's words for "liberality" to mean to distribute "liberally," the idea is more that gifts of money given by the individual to the needy should be for the single purpose of showing Christian love in meeting the needs of those lacking and not to gain merit before God or status before men. So hidden from men's eyes should these deeds be that Jesus said, "Let not your right hand know what your left hand is doing" (Mt 6:3). How different this sounds from so much Christian giving where everyone knows who the liberal donors are! I am reminded in contrast to this of the cornerstone plaque affixed to a large building complex now used by a well-known Christian organization in California: "Purchased by a Christian and donated to the glory of God."

Next, Paul refers to those who "lead." The Greek word for lead used here may mean "to care for." That "leading" and "caring for" are dual meanings for the word is explained by the fact that caring for the needs of people in the early church was the obligation of the elders or leading members (1 Th 5:12; 1 Ti 3:4-5; 5:17). The emphasis is not so much on authority or power as on pastoral care.[7] Jesus emphasized this aspect as the chief role of a leader (Lk 22:26). Caring for the flock is to be done with "diligence" or zeal, which may explain why a special recognition for this diligence is recommended by Paul elsewhere (1 Ti 5:17).

Finally, one who "shows mercy" as the expression of the Holy Spirit's gift should do these deeds cheerfully and brightly. Calvin's remark captures the spirit of the exhortation: "For as nothing gives more solace to the sick or to any one otherwise distressed, than to see men cheerful and prompt in assisting them; so to observe sadness in the face of those by whom assistance is given make them to feel themselves despised."[8]

While it is extremely encouraging in our day to find so many individual Christians exercising a variety of Spirit-ministered gifts, it is sad to see so few Christian churches that provide any structure in the church meetings for the spontaneous ministering of gifts to one another. To counteract this deficiency one church on the west coast has recently begun a Sunday evening meeting called a *Body-Life* service. After nearly a thousand people pack into the Peninsula Bible Church in Palo Alto, California, the leader gets things started by saying, "This is the family, the body of Christ. We need each other. Let's share." One after another,

7. TDNT, 6:702.
8. Cited by John Murray, *Epistle to the Romans*, 2:127.

persons all over the auditorium stand and speak. A divorced mother of three tells how God put food on the table that week. A glassy-eyed girl requests prayer for her older brother who is blowing his mind with LSD and won't stop. The leader asks a former "acid head" to go stand by her and lead out in prayer for the brother. A woman gives the keys for the family's second car to a student who has expressed a need for transportation for work. Other needs, insights, helps, prayers, comfort, and good news are shared, and at times laughter, applause, or hushed moments of anguish accompany the events. When the offering is taken, those in need may also take from the plate up to ten dollars![9] Somehow we feel that this must come closer to the New Testament meaning of the gifts than most of our churches have experienced.

## THE LAW OF LOVE APPLIED
### 12:9-21

At this point Paul seems to change the subject matter and offer a number of ethical injunctions or general rules for Christian conduct.[10] Each command appears permeated by the underlying principle of showing love first to the brethren in Christ (vv. 9-13), and then to all men, even to those who treat Christians as their enemies (vv. 14-21). In this section as well as the following, Paul seems to be integrating and applying Jesus' teaching found in the Sermon on the Mount (Mt 5-7) as well as selected Old Testament ethical injunctions. Two main overarching principles govern Christian conduct: love and peace. In these exhortations there is really no system of ethics propounded, but nevertheless all of life comes under the direction of the renewed mind in Christ (v. 2). Little comment is needed except at certain points in the exposition.

Paul heads the list with love, as he does elsewhere (Gal 5:22

---

9. Edward Plowman, *The Jesus Movement in America* (Elgin, Ill.: Cook, 1971).

10. The series of imperatives in English, "abhor," "cleave" are participles with imperative force in Greek and probably follow the Rabbinic Hebrew use of participles for expressing not direct commands but rules and codes (see C. K. Barrett, *The Epistle to the Romans,* p. 239). If this is a correct explanation of the linguistic phenomenon, then these commands could represent a Semitic source originating in a very early Jewish Christian church.

If love is true and genuine and not just a put-on or facade, then everything else to which Paul exhorts the church will follow. The great identifying mark of the Christian life-style and the final compelling apologetic for Christianity is the love that Christians have for one another (Jn 13:34, 35). This love must be especially visible to the world. One area of acid test is the way we walk toward other brothers who differ with us. We must truly regret our differences that cause friction among us and must show a costly love by practicing consciously our love for each other regardless of the inconvenience or loss to us personally or to our group.[11]

"Abhor [shrink back from] what is evil; cleave [stick in total devotion] to what is good" (v. 9) underscores the dual nature of the world in which Christians live. Christian love must at times constructively negate some things in the world and affirm others. Furthermore, this love should embrace fellow Christians as if they were members of the same family with all its emotional and affectionate ties (v. 10). Genuine love for others in our common family in Christ will incite us to "give preference to one another" or to "take the lead" in honoring the other before any honor comes our way (v. 10), each being readier than the other to recognize and honor God's gifts in a brother (Eph 3:8). This exhortation can have tremendous healing effects in the fractured church of today, especially if we will apply it to groups of Christians other than our own and in honor prefer them above ourselves!

Verse 11 contains three exhortations which seem to relate to the problem of Christian apathy. "Not lagging behind in diligence" is more literally "not hesitant in zeal" and relates to Christian enthusiasm in using God's gifts to multiply His harvest (Mt 25:26, 27; 2 Ti 1:6, 7). The same warning against discouragement appears elsewhere (Gal 6:9; Heb 12:3). To uncover this problem, the question could well be asked: Are there any issues in my life which I am concerned over? Have I ceased to get excited over anything anymore?

"Fervent in spirit" surely relates to both the former injunction and to the following command to serve the Lord. While "spirit"

11. Francis A. Schaeffer, *The Mark of the Christian* (Downers Grove, Ill.: Inter-Varsity, 1970).

could refer to the Holy Spirit, it is not necessary here, for the inner human spirit of the Christian is surely "set aglow" by the fire of the Spirit (Ac 18:25). The final order concerning "serving the Lord" suggests how this zeal is to be channeled to avoid apathy in our Christian lives. When the Christian becomes overly depressed in any type of work or service, and zeal ebbs, it may be due to the fact that the priority of the Lord's service has slipped from his mind. These are general exhortations designed to keep God's people from indolence and apathy.

Three further brief commands are linked together in verse 12: "rejoicing in hope, persevering in tribulation, devoted to prayer." Power for living now lies in the direction of the Christian's future hope (8:18-27). Because God has granted to us in His promises such a strong vision of His future kingdom and the resurrection, our present lives are to be lived as if this kingdom had already arrived.

Such living in hope will bring a radical criticism and judgment upon the present world order and result in the world's reaction and very often persecution. In these afflictions the believer must be steadfast and not relinquish his trust in God. No greater resource for strength in trials and joy in his hope can be found than in prayer which should be entered into as serious work, as part of the battle of spiritual warfare.

Being "devoted to" prayer emphasizes the persistence in prayer that distinguished the prayers of the early Christians from the merely religious performance of prayers of the contemporary Jews and pagans. "Devoted" to prayer catches well the force of the Greek word which means to stick diligently with something and attend to it (the same word is used in Eph 6:18; Ac 1:14; Lk 11:1-13; 18:1-8; Col 4:2).

Paul continues with the exhortation about "contributing to the needs of the saints" (v. 13). The force of the verb denotes "sharing in" or "partaking of" the needs of brothers in Christ. We are to feel a oneness, as in the same family, with those who suffer afflictions and deprivations for the name of Christ. When we truly follow this exhortation, it will be natural for us to also *meet* those needs if it is in our power.

If, on the other hand, these needy brethren come to us, we will receive them with open homes and hearts. "Practicing" hospitality does not quite catch the more intensive force of the verb which means "to actively pursue." Christian hospitality demands a special effort that goes beyond the mere inconvenience of non-Christian people; we cannot choose our time or our guests. Hospitality in the early church was a prime example of "contributing to the needs of the saints" (see also 1 Pe 4:9; Heb 13:2; 1 Ti 3:2; Titus 1:8). Perhaps we should see the test of this ministry today in terms of whether our homes are open to the more "hippie" type of young Christians or "Jesus people."

In verse 14 the character of thought abruptly changes. That there is a change can be noted for two reasons. First, the subject changes from general exhortations or commands stressing mainly relationships of Christians to other Christians to admonitions dealing with the Christian response to non-Christian attitudes and actions. Also, the grammatical structure of these verses changes from Greek participles to imperatives and infinitives.

"Bless those who persecute you; bless, and curse not" (v. 14) reminds us definitely of our Lord's words (Mt 5:44; Lk 6:28). Such a response demands the exercise of radical Christian love expressed toward one who has made himself our enemy by persecuting us. To bless means more than mere words since the utterance must come from the heart and will be followed by the appropriate action as occasion affords. When we "rejoice with those who rejoice, and weep with those who weep" (v. 15), we as Christians identify with all men in our common humanity as fellow human beings. We must and should be truly able to empathize with them after the example of our Lord (Lk 15:1-2). The early church father, Chrysostom, poignantly observed how much easier it is to weep with others than to rejoice with them. It is at the point of a man's sorrows and joys that he is most deeply himself. At this point the Christian is to identify in love with him.

In verse 16, Paul continues by admonishing Christians to cultivate a loving harmony and practice of humility in the company of non-Christians. "Do not be haughty in mind, but associate with the lowly" is a difficult passage and unfortunately ambiguous in the Greek. Does the "lowly" refer to men or things? If the latter, then the thought is that we are not to cherish selfish ambitions, but to give ourselves over to humble tasks (Phil 4:11; 1 Ti 6:8, 9). If "lowly" refers to men, then the sense is that we are to give ourselves over to association with the less attractive, more lowly people in the world. There is no final way to decide between the two views. Both are worthy Christian goals. In either case one line of thought would lead to the other.

The force of the exhortation, "Do not be wise in your own estimation" is that we must not be conceited (Pr 3:7). Such words strike at the very heart of an opinionated person who cherishes his own ideas and judgments as if they themselves were the absolute truth and refuses to acknowledge the opinions and thoughts of others. Furthermore, we should not be misled by our own preferences which often incline toward that which flatters our pride, namely, the distinguished and brilliant. There is a way of clinging to the truth which is no more than a way of clinging to oneself.

Finally, in verses 17-21 of the chapter, Paul interacts more specifically with the question of Christian response to hostility from non-Christians. As in the teaching of Jesus concerning nonviolence and nonretaliation (Mt 5:38-42), Paul's concern is with the question of private, personal, and individual relationships and reactions. In chapter 13 he will consider what response toward hostility and evil is correct for civil authorities.

Love will never retaliate or "pay back" blow for blow for harm done (Pr 17:13), but on the contrary will "respect [take thought] for what is right [Gk. means "good"] in the sight of all men" (v. 17). Christian conduct should be recognizably commendable before non-Christian men (1 Th 5:15; 2 Co 8:21). Many Christians today, in contrast, are far more concerned with how their behavior strikes their Christian friends than whether it is acceptable to the non-Christian consensus.

This rule of behavior does not mean that the Christian will turn to the world for his norms of conduct, but in seeking the will of God for each ethical situation, he will consider what is right and just in the sight of all men as part of the basis for his decision (v. 2). In practice, the believer must weigh the consequences of whatever action he takes against the effects of the testimony that results to the nonbelieving community for or against the Christian message (1 Co 10:31-32; Mt 5:16). This principle takes into account that God's law is operative in the hearts of all men, however dimly they perceive or recognize His norms as they formulate their concepts of right and wrong (2:15). The Christian, however, is always to obey God's law instead of man's wherever conflict arises.

By so acting, the interests of peace and good will among men are promoted (v. 18). There is, however, a qualification: "If possible, so far as it depends on you," or if the possibility of peace can be brought about by you. Peace cannot be secured at the cost of God's truth or if others refuse to cooperate (Mt 10:34-36; Lk 12:51-53; Ja 3:17). The Christian should do everything in his power to be the reconciling salt in the hostilities between men in the world. If conflict arises where the Christian is involved, let it only arise because of the Christian's stand for the truth of God and justice. Strife or conflict should never be sought or initiated by the Christian.

In verses 19-21 the apostle answers a possible objection to his peace way of life (v. 18). Someone might say, won't this approach play into the hands of evil men, favoring their scheme and allowing them to go unchecked in their wickedness? Wouldn't it be better to set them straight forcefully and put an end to their injustice? Paul says, no! The essence of sin in human relations is for an individual man to assume the place of God and take justice into his own hands. A man cannot presume to do this, because not only is he limited in his information and understanding, but when his own personal interests have been hurt he will invariably distort justice in favor of his own selfish concerns.

Therefore, the individual Christians must not try to "get even" with the other person who has wronged him. Instead he must commit himself in trust to the administration of God's justice upon the unjust person, that is, "God's wrath" (2:5, 8; 3:5; 5:9; 9:22). God's wrath is being presently directed toward evil doers both directly (1:18-25) and indirectly through the civil authorities (13:4, "wrath") and will be completely manifest in the future final judgment (Ro 2:5, 6; Rev. 20:11-15). Paul quotes Deuteronomy 32:35 to support this principle of nonretaliation which should be the rule of God's people.

But the Christian must do more than be passive toward personal animosity; he should also take positive steps to manifest that he does not harbor vengeance against the offender. While he does not pay back evil for evil, he does pay back good in return for the harm: "If your enemy is hungry, feed him, and if he is thirsty, give him a drink" (v. 20). Here Paul seems to call to mind Jesus' admonition to love the enemy (Mt 5:44 and Lk 6:27), but he actually quotes Proverbs 25:21, 22. "Burning coals upon his head" does not refer to coals of judgment (hence a way of getting back at the other) but the fires of shame and remorse burning the conscience of the offender and hopefully bringing about repentance and reconciliation to the offended. By following this unnatural but loving course of action, the Christian will not be conquered by evil men in his life of promoting peace (v. 18). He will instead conquer such evil fostered against him by good (acts of love) toward the evildoer, more than he could through acts of vengeance (v. 21). Thus evil is more permanently dealt with when the heart of the evildoer is changed and his resentment overcome than if he were merely brought to justice.

THE CHRISTIAN AND CIVIL AUTHORITIES

13:1-7

It is important at the first in this highly controversial passage to establish the link, if any, in thought with the preceding section. This teaching on government appears somewhat abruptly (without connecting particle) between two exhortations pertaining to the exercise of Christian love and peace (12:9-21 and 13:8-10). Arguments can be advanced for a logical connection with the preceding in either the idea of "vengeance" and "God's wrath" (12:19 with 13:4); or with the thought of not being conformed to the world or any of its institutions (12:2); or as answering the problem as to whether the Christian is to view the state as evil because it renders evil for evil, which the Christian is not to do.

While these logical connections may not be absent, they are largely matters of conjecture. Actually the local historical conditions in Rome itself may have had more to do with the inclusion of this section on civil authorities than the previous subject material. Such a view would also be in keeping with the more spontaneous nature of the exhortations in chapters 12-16. In any case we should not think of this section on civil government as a parenthesis in his exposition.

Adopting the historical explanation may be better for several reasons. In the first place there is good evidence that, at the time Paul wrote Romans (early A.D. 57), there was considerable hostility mounting between Rome and the Jews. In A.D. 49 the emperor Claudius finally had to expel all the Jews from Rome due to the continual disturbances and riots caused by one Chrestus (or Christ).[12] A further inscription of the times may show that this trouble was caused by the preaching of the resurrection of Jesus in Rome by believing Jews and the countercharge of unbelieving Jews that the body of Jesus was removed from its tomb by the disciples (Mt 28:11-15). This tomb-robbery allegation could explain why the trouble resulted in Rome in connection with "Chrestus" between Jewish Christians and nonbelieving Jews and also why Claudius wrote an ordinance about this same time (curiously found in Nazareth) forbidding tampering with graves on punishment of death.[13]

In addition, Jewish revolutionary activities (by zealots) against Rome during this period are well-known. Since Jesus was a Jewish Messiah, the Roman government was likely to suspect all followers of Jesus as having revolutionary tendencies. Therefore, any insubordination to the authorities among groups of Christians could be interpreted as a revolutionary threat to Roman rule on the part of the whole Christian movement.

Furthermore, there is evidence that due to either pagan or Jewish backgrounds certain Christians entertained perverted theological notions of Christ's kingship and lordship and its relation

12. C. W. Barrett, ed. *The New Testament Background,* p. 14. Acts 18:2 records that the Jew, Aquila, and his wife, Priscilla (Prisca in Ro 16:3) were expelled by Claudius from Rome. They were probably Christians before they met Paul.

13. Ibid., p. 15; also E. M. Blaiklock, *The Century of the New Testament* (London: Tyndale Press, n.d.), p. 42. The inscription was discovered in 1932.

to the kingdoms of this world (see Mt 22:17).[14] Was obedience to Christ as King compatible with obedience to the civil institutions? This question also involved the further problem of the extension of Christian liberty under Christ's lordship to include freedom from all other authorities of any kind (1 Pe 2:13-17).

In the actual text of 13:1-7 four general principles concerning the relationship of the Christian to government can be summarized: (1) there is a binding Christian responsibility toward the authority of the governing rulers as well as toward the authority of Christ; (2) human government is a *divine* institution; (3) the purpose of government is twofold: to promote the good in society, and to restrain and punish criminals; and (4) loyalty in general to the government and support of its needs should be the correct attitude of every Christian.

More specifically, Paul first states in verses 1 and 2 that all Christians ("every person") with no exceptions are to be obedient to the "governing authorities." They are to do this because all past rulers ("no authority except from God") and present government officials ("those which exist") have been appointed by the will of God (Dan 2:21; 4:17, 35; Jn 19:11). Furthermore, to resist the government agent in the discharge of his duties is to resist the command of God and incur, therefore, God's judgment ministered through the penalty imposed by the authorities (v. 2).

The "authorities" are most certainly the government officials in the Roman commonwealth.[15] At the time of Paul's writing (early A.D. 57), Nero was emperor of Rome (A.D. 54-68). Though it is true that Nero was cruel, lustful, and murderously vicious, yet he had the aid of two provincials (Burrus and Seneca) who were relatively honest and promoted a model government during the first five years of Nero's reign (during the time Paul wrote this letter). It is amazing that the apostle wrote these words on

14. See H. P. Liddon, *Explanatory Analysis of St. Paul's Epistle to the Romans,* p. 246, for illustrations from Jewish and Ebionite sources to the effect that government authorities were the expression of the evil and devilish power of the universe.

15. Although Oscar Cullman (*The State in the New Testament* [New York: Scribner, 1956], pp. 93ff.) has shown that philologically the word "powers" or "authorities" in Paul's writings has a dual reference to both angelic powers and government rulers (see Col 1:20; 2:15), it does not seem to fit the evidence in this passage. (See Murray, 2:252ff. for criticism of Cullmann.)

obedience to government after being himself recently mistreated by the Roman authorities at Philippi (Ac 16:37). Peter also wrote much of the same type of exhortation to Christians later in the reign of Nero (1 Pe 2:13-17, c. A.D. 64). "Will receive condemnation" is more literally, shall receive "judgment" from the rulers, not external damnation (v. 2).

Paul goes on to describe the reason why the punitive power given to the civil authority can be used (vv. 3-4). God has appointed government officials to a two-fold duty which reflects the general purpose of the state: (1) government must not destroy or subvert the good of society but protect and promote it: "do what is good, and you will have praise from the same" (v. 3); "for it is a minister of God to you for good" (v. 4); and (2) the civil power must deter crime and bring to punishment those who foster evil in society: "it does not bear the sword for nothing; for it is a minister of God, an avenger who brings wrath upon the one who practices evil," (v. 4). Christians who do good and not evil should have no fear of the civil powers.

"Praise" from the ruler (v. 3) simply implies approval with no necessary reward involved. Evangelicals could do better in emphasizing this theme rather than always the punitive aspect of government. "Minister of God" (two times, v. 4) refers to the discharge of God's appointed civil authority (vv. 1, 2) and has no reference to implications concerning the salvation of the ruler. Such a term strongly counteracts any tendency to attribute evil to the existence of the state *per se*, as some are advocating in our day. That the ruler is a minister of God "to you" argues that government exists for the good of the Christian community, as well as for the non-Christian (v. 4). The state, then, is not just an entity for unbelievers, but God's grace to the church is in some measure mediated through its protection and good benefits.

The "sword" that the ruler bears refers to more than the mere symbol of his authority but also suggests his right to wield it to enforce justice, and if need be to inflict death (Mt 26:52; Ac 12:2; 16:27; Heb 11:34, 37).[16] "For nothing" means for no purpose or

16. The "sword" is the power possessed by all higher magistrates of inflicting the death penalty for certain crimes and is known technically as *ius gladii* (Tacitus, *Histories* 3:68, cited by Barrett, *The Epistle to the Romans*, p. 247).

for no use. The ruler does not just wear the sword for effect merely, but he may also use it in administering justice. The ruler is further described in this service to God as an "avenger" (note that this is the same Greek word as "vengeance" in 12:19) for wrath (i.e., God's wrath, 12:19). What Paul expressly forbids to the individual Christian (vengeance) is here attributed rightfully to the civil powers. There is no inconsistency in this because God's method of dealing with evil is not through individual vengeance but through His own justice as ministered by the state, though the state is recognizably imperfect and occasionally in error.

We understand from this that the government ruler has authority from God to promote the good and punish evil as God's own servant in these civil matters. Such recognition lays a two-fold moral obligation upon Christians to comply with civil authorities (v. 5). First, because to resist the state by doing evil would incur their "wrath" or force which, as we have argued, is in fact an expression of God's vengeance upon evil (v. 5). Second, our "conscience" toward God would smite us because we have violated His ordained authority over our lives in this area (v. 5).

It should be remembered that our conscience is not a standard in itself but involves a mechanism that is set by knowledge of the right and wrong obtained from an external source. The Christian conscience is to be developed by God's Word, His Creation order, and the promptings of the Holy Spirit. Therefore, whenever the civil power commands us to violate God's will, we must refuse on the same grounds of conscience toward God (Ac 4:19, 20; 5:29). Peter says, "Submit yourselves for the Lord's sake" (1 Pe 2:13). It is this matter of conscience toward God that leaves open the possibility of resistance and even disobedience to government.

Finally, Paul pushes one step further and suggests that since government is ordained by God, the Christian should participate in its continued existence by supporting the various needs of government, such as taxes, tolls, duties, assessments, and respect for officials as servants of God (vv. 6-7). "Devoting themselves" to taxes (v. 6) is the same word used in 12:12 for the Christians being "devoted" to prayer. If Christians would exercise the same concern over prayer that the Internal Revenue Service does over collecting our taxes, no telling what might happen in today's church! "Tax" is the direct tax such as income and real estate tax, while "custom" refers to indirect taxes on goods such as sales and custom taxes. This description in no way limits or justifies a particular form of tax or the amount assessed.

It seems clear that Paul's position on the relationship of the disciple of Christ to the governing authorities is the same as that of Jesus. Both are opposed to the zealot's revolutionary concept. In his oft-quoted words, Jesus deftly balances the two authorities, "Render to Caesar the things that are Caesar's; and to God the things that are God's" (Mt 22:21).

Paul's theological position concerning the civil authorities leaves several contemporary questions unanswered. We can do no more here than attempt a passing comment or two.

WHAT IS THE BEST FORM OF GOVERNMENT?

Paul does not commend or condemn any particular form of government nor does the rest of the New Testament. From a Christian perspective, any form of government is better than anarchy and as such is worthy of our loyal support. We must remember that Roman government with its wedding of the pagan gods and emperor worship presented no more of a special problem to Christians in the first century than would living as a Christian under an atheistic form of communism today.

It should also be noted that Paul didn't know about participatory democracies or republics, since Rome did not allow all of its subjects to vote or run for office or participate in decisions that affected the people. If such had been Paul's situation, he might have exhorted much more of a positive involvement in government than simply paying taxes and complying with the rulers. Which form of government is better than others must be settled on the level of political and economic theory informed by Scripture but not on the theological level.

SHOULD GOVERNMENT POLICY EVER BE CRITICIZED?

Is it possible to be loyal to the civil authorities in obedience to Romans 13 and at the same time be critical of certain acts or policies of government officials? Apparently Jesus felt free to criticize not only the Jewish civil leaders (Jn 18:23), but also the Roman ruler Herod Antipas in referring to him as the "fox" (Lk 13:32). Paul likewise accused one of the members of a grand jury, who commanded him to be hit on the mouth, of being a "whitewashed wall," although he apologized when he learned that the man who issued the order was the high priest (Ac 23:1-5).

These examples are few but are sufficient to show that the principle of a critical attitude toward certain civil acts and policies is not foreign to Christianity. Such criticism should always be aimed at improving and not subverting the government or aimed at questioning whether a particular officer rightly represents a government. The Christian must say both yes to the state and no to the state. A Christianity tied too closely to the civil authorities soon finds itself being used as a tool to sanction the particular policies and acts of a government which uses the church to win citizen approval.

WHAT ABOUT CIVIL DISOBEDIENCE?

It is clear that the New Testament teaches that obedience to God always takes priority over obedience to the state regardless of the consequences (Ac 4:19, 20; 5:29). While a direct command of the state to disobey a direct command of God—say in the case of idolatrous worship—presents little problem, the question arises whether resistance and even disobedience to the government may be the right action when our conscience toward God dictates to us in less direct matters. For example, Paul apparently resisted, or even disobeyed, the Roman official's command to leave prison secretly because he judged that he had been treated unjustly by the Philippian civil authorities (Ac 16:35-40). He could not have had a direct command from God to not leave prison secretly.

There are many vexing questions in regard to civil disobedience, and conscientious Christians have been divided over this issue down through history.[17] This much can be said. Paul does not

17. Daniel B. Stevick, *Civil Disobedience and the Christian* (New York: Seabury, 1969). Stevick argues that the scriptural ambiguity on this question has pervaded the church from earliest times to the present.

qualify his request for obedience to the civil powers in Romans 13. However, he does indicate that the proper role of government is in promoting good and punishing evil, and refers to the role of "conscience" toward God in our actions. It can be assumed that if either of these two conditions are not met there is ground for resistance or even disobedience. The state is not absolute in its demands over us, nor is it infallible or always on the side of justice. The question of when and how the state should be resisted or disobeyed will never find unanimous consensus among Christians. The question must be constantly studied and discussed as we bring all of our decisions to the bar of careful scriptural examination and Christian conscience. Whatever action is taken must be responsible and conscientiously fully Christian.

Should a christian ever participate in political revolution?

This question is extremely important in a day of worldwide revolutionary movements, especially among young people., Political revolution is a more extreme form of civil disobedience directed at the destruction of the established structure of a particular form of government and the ultimate replacement of it by a new form of rule. Paul does give instruction as to what a Christian should do when a revolution has occurred: "Be in subjection to the governing authorities" (13:1). At what point this new government is the "governing authority" he does not discuss because such discussion lies more in the area of moral and political thought than theological direction for Christian behavior.

Furthermore, Paul indicates that the ideal government functions as God's servant when it promotes "good" and resists "evil" (13:3). If, in the judgment of a majority of its people, the existing government is largely suppressing good and promoting evil, has the civil authority abdicated its divine orders and thus proven no longer worthy of the Christian's obedience?

Whatever our answer to these vexing questions for the Christian conscience, it must be affirmed that because our ultimate (though not exclusive) loyalty belongs to the kingdom of God, we can never be identified totally with either a proposed revolution or the established form of government powers. Our position in Christ will lead us to be critical of, but not aloof from, all human move-

ments. There can be no "Christian" revolution. One should also
realize that much of the revolutionary movement in our times
arises from a Marxist philosophy of history and not a Christian
world-view.

### DOES PAUL ADVISE THE CHRISTIAN TO GO TO WAR?

It should be clear from what has been said on the exegesis of
the text of Romans 13:1-7 that Paul is not talking about whether
governments have the divine right to wage war or not. The
"sword" is the right to punish offenders of the civil government
even by death. Whether this right also extends to punishing evil-
doers who assault the government from without can only be an
inference from this passage and not a direct teaching.

From very earliest times the church has been divided over
whether killing in warfare under obedience to one's government
constitutes a violation of the sixth commandment against killing.
One group of Christians (pacifist) sees such killing as disobedience to God's will and refuses to participate; another group (believers in a just war) believes that governments must from time
to time defend themselves in punishing the evildoer through warfare and have therefore a right to expect its citizens to obey and
bring the offenders to justice by whatever means is necessary.

While Paul does seem to consent to the legitimate use of force
by the civil ruler within his realm, which presents a problem to
the pacifist position against violence of any kind, he does not for-
bid or justify killing in warfare. This difficult question must be
settled by bringing other factors to bear including scriptural principles (Old and New Testament) and moral concerns. If I as a
Christian agree that obedience to the state involves going to war,
this does not relieve me of bringing appropriate moral criticism
to bear on the military activities of my country.

### FURTHER INSTRUCTIONS ON LOVE, VIGILANCE, AND HOLINESS
#### 13:8-14

In this section Paul shows how the great command of Christ
concerning love relates to the divine commands under the old
covenant. He argues that the old and the new are mutually

complementary, the former hinting of the latter, and the latter revealing the former (vv. 8-10). At the close of the chapter Paul turns to exhortations to holiness motivated from a consideration of the nearness of Christ's return and the consequent urgency to act (vv. 11-14).

In verse 8 Paul calls upon Christians to "owe nothing to anyone," which is understood by some to refer back to verse 7 concerning paying our taxes. In any case this exhortation refers to unpaid debts and not to borrowing money (Ex 22:25; Mt 5:42; Lk 6:35). All of our obligations are to be paid up except one: the perpetual debt of Christian love to one another. This sole perpetual obligation is not at variance with the obligations of the divine commands of Moses, because "he who loves his neighbor has fulfilled the law." The neighbor (v. 9), who often becomes the one like-minded to ourselves, is literally, "the other one who is different" from us (Gk. *heteros*, the other who is different). This guards Christian love from mere mutual admiration.

In verses 9 and 10, Paul explains further the connection between the law and Christian love. He cites the following commandments of the Mosaic tables as the epitome of law (the order varies somewhat): adultery, killing, stealing, and coveting. He says that these and any other commands of God (positive and negative) are summed up in the statement, "You shall love your neighbor as yourself" (v. 9, from Lev 19:18; Mt 22:39-40). Paul's point simply is that the essence or chief point of all the commands is to promote loving action toward the other person. He is stressing that law and love serve the one and the same end, to do no harm to the other person (v. 10).

To pit love against law as some have done in our day is to miss Paul's whole point.[18] Where love prevails the things which the law forbids do not occur (see Gal 5:23). Note carefully that the apostle does not institute a new legalism of "love–righteousness"

18. Joseph Fletcher, *Situation Ethics*, pp. 69-75. Fletcher's strong antithesis between law and love violates Paul's whole emphasis and lies at the heart of Fletcher's strong relativistic love-only ethic. As Edward L. Long, Jr. has noted, Fletcher's approach borders strongly on a new legalism which has replaced the old Pharisaic "works/righteousness" with the new "context/righteousness." (See Paul Ramsey and Gene H. Outka, eds., *Norm and Context in Christian Ethics* [New York: Scribner, 1968], pp. 281ff).

to merit justification as the situation ethicist does, but in Paul's teaching the fulfilling of the law is a valid divine expression of love for the neighbor. Since the law required love to the other person, Paul teaches that "love is the fulfillment [or fullness] of the law" (v. 10). It is only love that makes the law fulfill its purpose. The Christian who walks continually in love fulfills all the demands of the law.

The thought changes in verses 11-14. The apostle turns to a final ethical exhortation pertaining to the urgency of adorning the life of holiness in Christ. Verse 11 gives a further reason for doing all the exhortations in chapters 12 and 13; it is the kind of "time" we live in. The word Paul uses for time (Gk. *kairos*) means not chronological succession of time but kind of time, season, or quality of time. In the New Testament it often has an eschatological usage (Mk 13:33; Lk 21:8; Ac 1:7; 1 Th 5:1; 1 Ti 4:1; 1 Pe 1:5; Rev 11:18). According to the New Testament, we are living in the eschatological "last days" (Ac 2:17; 2 Ti 3:1; Heb 1:2; 1 Jn 2:18), not chronologically but qualitatively. This "last days" kind of time began with the first coming of Christ and continues until His second coming. "Last days" are the days of the imminent consummation of all things and the manifestation of our full salvation (8:23) in the kingdom of God (the coming of the "day" into the world). Each day brings us closer to this consummation.

Since we live on the edge, or brink, of this new day, our conduct must be in keeping with this momentary end event. We must wake up and not live or "sleep" as if the character of the time were different (Mt 24:42-44). Christ's coming was always "imminent" to the church, not in the sense that it was soon to happen, but from the standpoint that nothing major needed to occur before Christ could return. Paul and the early church (as in every generation) may have thought the coming was soon (1 Co 7:29-31), they may have even later revised their estimate (2 Ti 4:6-8), but they still maintained their view of imminency. They believed that Christ might still come at any moment (Rev 2:25; 3:11; 22:20).

Since the character of the coming consummation is "light" and "day," the proper response is to live in the light as if the day had already dawned ("properly," v. 13, really means "appropriately"). This requires arousing ourselves and putting off the night clothes of darkness: "carousing and drunkenness . . . sexual promiscuity and sensuality (moral corruptness) . . . strife and jealousy" (v. 13). Finally, we are to put on the "day" clothes consisting of the "armor of light" (v. 12), which Paul elsewhere states to be faith, love, and hope (1 Th 5:8, 9); or goodness, righteousness, and truth (Eph 5:7-10)—weapons for conflict against the forces of spiritual darkness. The figure of changing clothes is, in good Hebrew tradition, an appeal to make an inward and spiritual change (Is 61:10; Zec 3:3).

But nothing is so inclusive as the word in verse 14: "Put on the Lord Jesus Christ" (see Gal 3:27). To put on Christ means to live in conformity to His mind and will (12:2), which is the natural outworking of our identification and union with Christ in His death and resurrection (6:1-10). To "make provision for the flesh" is to make plans for satisfying the selfish and sinful desires of the flesh. John's emphasis is the same when he says, "we shall be like Him. . . . Every one who has this hope fixed on Him purifies himself, just as He is pure" (1 Jn 3:3).

Historically, some importance can be attached to this section in that the great theologian, Augustine, was led to a personal acceptance of Jesus Christ on the basis of these last two verses as he tearfully meditated under a fig tree (*Confessions*, Book VIII).

It is sad to find in our day that much "prophetic" teaching and preaching stresses the chronological timetable approach and lacks the true sense of the apocalyptic force of the Pauline and New Testament emphasis.[19] And yet this later type of preaching is greatly needed in today's apathetic and morally weak Christian church.

---

19. The prophetic or eschatological may be distinguished slightly from the apocalyptic by understanding the prophetic to be viewing the future from the standpoint of the present, whereas the apocalyptic views the present from the ground of the future. This is often overlooked. The NT has both perspectives, but most preaching on prophecy today reflects only the former. A return to the more biblical view could have great significance, especially to more apathetic forms of Christianity in our day. (See Carl E. Braaten, *Christ and Counter-Christ* [Philadelphia: Fortress, 1972].)

CHRISTIAN FREEDOM AND CHRISTIAN LOVE
14:1–15:13

With the previous section Paul has concluded a series of ethical injunctions relating to personal, church, world, state, and Christian holiness. In chapters 14 and 15 (first part) the thought changes to a consideration of a special problem existing in the church due to the diverse cultural backgrounds of certain converts to Christianity. The problem may have been especially intensified by the presence in the church of Rome (also at Corinth—1 Co 8-10) of both Jewish and Gentile Christians. The Jewish minority in the church may have been reluctant both (1) to give up certain ascetic rules such as to eat no flesh (v. 2) and to drink no wine (v. 21), and (2) to give up some of the Jewish feasts and fasts (v. 5). However, there is no evidence that these people were exclusively, or even primarily, Jewish in background.

This problem over religious and cultural background in the churches of Rome and Corinth should not be confused with the more serious problems involving certain Judaizing teachers at Galatia (Gal 5:2), or the Jewish Gnostic teachers at Colosse (Col 2:16, 17, 21). These latter cases involve doctrinal distortions and warrant no toleration on Paul's part, while the Roman problem calls for a sympathetically patient attitude from the apostle. Furthermore, the problem at Corinth of eating food and drink sacrificed to idols does not seem to be the same issue dealt with here in Romans, even though both issues resulted in an unchristian spirit of alienation. Paul exhorts each brother to walk in love toward the other who differs with him in this matter (14:15).

These chapters have special pertinence to Christians today who have different opinions over the religious and moral significance of certain practices which are not specifically mentioned in the Bible. To see exactly how Paul deals with these problems is of the utmost importance to us in preserving the love and unity in the Christian family.

More specifically, in the church at Rome there was a group which, because of religious conviction and conscience, wanted to refrain from the eating of certain foods (meat and wine, v. 21) and to consider "one day better than another" (v. 5). It should be clear from what follows that Paul is not talking about any specific commands of God or biblical prohibitions such as adultery, lying, and idolatry. The argument was over the use of certain material things and the observance of social customs. This group was considered "weak" by the majority in the congregation who had no qualms of conscience in these matters. The problem then was how the church should respond to this minority opinion.

We are not told why this group held these opinions. However, there is good reason, based on the similar problem in Corinth (1 Co 8-10), to believe that the abstainers from meat and wine had associated these substances with their former idolatrous worship and drunken life. The "day" problem, on the other hand, might be related to Jewish converts who felt compelled to continue the observance of the Sabbath day. Paul clearly agrees with the majority that the scruples of the weak are baseless. He is convinced, out of his relationship to Christ, that "nothing is unclean in itself" (v. 14). The apostle thinks these things are of small matter to Christian faith, but because the problem has threatened the unity of the church, he must deal with it at length.

THE PRINCIPLE OF MUTUAL ACCEPTANCE (14:1-4)

What should the majority in the church do? The answer is clear. They who are strong should "accept" (welcome, accept fully) the weak (v. 1). Even though the weak in faith has qualms about certain matters, he is a full member of the body of Christ and "God has accepted him" (v. 3). But the strong should not receive him for the purpose of debating and changing his practice over his scruples ("his opinions," v. 1). An attitude like this on the part of the strong would only fan the problem into a larger fire of division. Instead, there should be mutual acceptance of each other without either snobbery on the part of the strong or criticism on the part of the weak (vv. 3-4). It should be to the glory of the church that we accept one another fully as we are without trying to press one another into one particular mold. Any such forced conformity is expressly forbidden in these exhortations.

### THE PRINCIPLE OF INNER MOTIVATIONS (14:5-9)

In verses 5-8, in contrast to petty divisions over social customs, Paul stresses what really is important in the Christian life. Whether we eat meat or do not eat meat is incidental. What is important is the inward motivation of our actions. We are to develop personal convictions before the Lord on everything we do: "Let each man be fully convinced in his own mind" (v. 5). In the following verses (6-9) appears one of the strongest passages in the New Testament on the lordship of Jesus Christ over the individual Christian's life ("Lord" occurs 7 times). Both the strong and the weak are motivated out of devotion to Christ in their behavior, which is evidenced in that they both "give thanks" to God for what they allow or abstain from (v. 6). In verses 7 and 8 there is further emphasis on the possession of the believer by Christ and the consequent attitude of the Christian toward the issue of his whole life and toward the issue of his death. We no longer live to ourselves but we live to Him who died and rose again that He might be our Lord in life and our Lord in death (v. 9).

### THE PRINCIPLE OF PRESUMPTIVE JUDGMENT (14:10-12)

When either the strong despises the weak, or the weak condemns the strong, one has presumptively judged the other. All judgment in these matters must be left to the Lord Himself who alone will know whether or not the motivation behind our actions was indeed to honor Him. Paul appeals to Isaiah 45:23 to support his point of the future, universal judgment of all believers (v. 11). In that day we will not be held accountable for others, but we will only be responsible for ourselves to Him alone, "each one of us shall give account of himself to God" (Ro 14:12; 1 Co 3:11-15; 2 Co 5:10).

### THE PRINCIPLE OF THE LIMITATION OF FREEDOM IN CHRISTIAN LOVE (14:13-23)

Paul now turns to exhort the strong concerning their conduct which their love for the weak demands. When the strong uses his freedom, he is not wrong in his position (v. 14), but he must

never consciously allow his freedom to jeopardize the spiritual
life and growth of a brother in Christ. Though nothing (material)
is evil (unclean) in itself, it may be viewed as evil by a person
whose mind is more influenced by his cultural background than
by the truth of God's creation taught in Scripture (Mk 7:15).

One of my young daughters brought home the suggestion from
school of how an avocado seed could be put in a glass of water
to sprout and then subsequently planted. In a week or so we
noticed a strong, repulsive odor coming from the kitchen. After
much looking, we found the source. Right, it was the avocado
seed, which had rotted and become rancid. Mother threw out
the seed and thoroughly scalded the pretty, flowered juice glass.
But until this day no one in our family will drink anything out
of this glass. It is perfectly clean, but in our minds it is associated
with the rotten avocado seed so we cannot comfortably use it
any longer.

The real issue revolves around the meaning of the "stumbling
block" or "offense" (vv. 13, 20, 21). What is it that the strong
Christian creates for the weak by the use of his freedom which
causes the weak to "be hurt" (v. 15), destroyed or torn down (vv.
15, 20), and even condemned (v. 23)? The language used is
much too strong to refer simply, as it is commonly explained, to
the displeasure felt in the heart of the weak when they see another
Christian doing something which they feel is evil. The weak must
in some way be emboldened by the example of the strong to actually *do something* against his conscientious conviction of the
good, and thus his conscience is violated and "hurt" over his own
sin. Since such an action is done not out of faith but against his
faith, it brings God's judgment into his life and ruins his relationship to Christ (v. 23). He does not lose his salvation but
damages his personal relationship with God through sin.

The strong, then, must consider the gravity of the consequence
for the weak of his example. If he fails to take thought in this
manner for his brother, he is not walking in responsible love and
thus sins himself against Christ (vv. 15, 20). Note that the
stumbling block is not the mere displeasure which another brother
may have over my behavior, but the temptation for him to go beyond what his faith approves and to sin by abandoning his con-

victions. He has done this thing not to please Christ, as I have done, but because of desire for pleasure or convenience. The weak has misunderstood my example.

But what about the freedom we, the strong in faith, have in Christ? If we accommodate our behavior to weaker Christians, won't we have to give up our freedom which Christ wants us to exercise? Furthermore, shouldn't the Christian show his freedom to the world and thereby show his faith? Paul says that the faith which we (the strong) have, we are to keep between ourselves and God privately (v. 22). And it is not the display of our freedom that commends our faith to the world but our practice of responsible love (Jn 13:35). We are God's representatives to the world, not in matters of freedom over food and drink, but in matters of the kingdom of God. The kingdom is God's rule over us. What are the issues, then, of this kingdom? Paul answers, "Righteousness and peace and joy in the Holy Spirit" (v. 17). One who is thus emphasizing the justice of God in life's human relations and peace between men and who thrives on the inner joy produced by the Holy Spirit has found the really important essence of Christianity before God and man (v. 18).

THE PRINCIPLE OF LIVING TO PLEASE OTHERS (15:1-6)

Not only are the strong to walk in responsible love for their weaker brothers, but they are to help them by bearing (along with) their weaknesses (infirmities) even when it is distasteful, "and not just to please ourselves" (15:1, 2). The example of Christ provides Paul with further reason to support his exhortation (v. 3). The whole human life of Jesus is summed up as a willing humiliation whereby He Himself bore the reproaches of the ungodly against God (Ps 69:9). Paul's point seems to be that whatever inconveniences or reproach the strong may have to endure in order to please their weaker brothers and thus edify them, it can never compare with the inconvenience and reproach which our Saviour endured in order to bring us eternal benefit.

Such Scriptures as Paul has been quoting provide the Christian with instructions in "perseverance" (steadfastness) and "encouragement" (v. 4). Just how this is related to the context is not clear. Perhaps Paul means that by learning from the Scriptures that God is aware of our reproaches and lot and that He supplies what we need to be steadfast—we have hope (encouragement) in His ultimate plan and providence. In any case, the character of God is found in the Scriptures which strike the note of hope in those who hear them speak.

Finally, by relying on such graces which come to us from the God who is revealed to us in the Scriptures, we can glorify God for His mercy to us with a united voice of praise free from condemning attitudes toward one another (15:5-6). Rather than criticizing each other and being perpetually suspicious of one another, we ought, according to Christ's will for us, to seek together the glory of God in all our relationships.

CHRIST AND THE GENTILES (15:7-13)

These verses reflect again the fact that there was racial prejudice in the church at Rome. Jewish believers could not overcome their backgrounds of discrimination against the Gentiles. Accustomed to thinking of non-Jews as "sinners of Gentiles" and "dogs," Jews, even though affirming Jesus as Lord, still could not accept their Gentile brethren as fully as they did their own. Paul speaks sharply to this issue and encourages them to put away all such attitudes and actions. He says, "accept one another, just as Christ also accepted us to the glory of God" (v. 7). You are to treat the other person, no matter how different he is from you, in the same way Christ treated you. There can be no racial discrimination where this truth is taken seriously and obeyed.

Turning to the ministry of Jesus, Paul asserts the reason why Christ confined His labors to the Jewish people. It was not because of favoritism, but for the purpose of fulfilling the oath-ratified, covenant promises made to the Jewish patriarchs (v. 8). "Circumcision" was the covenant seal given to Abraham and his descendants in hope of the realization of the promise of a seed in whom all the world be blessed (Gal 3:16; 4:9-31).

Furthermore, contained in the original patriarchal promises was the promise of universal blessing to all men (Gen 22:17, 18; Gal 3:8). Therefore, Christ's ministry to the Jews ("circumcision") was not only to prove God's faithfulness to His Word but also "for the Gentiles to glorify God for His mercy" to them also (v. 9). Paul proceeds in verses 9-12 to string together Old Testament quotations that predicted the blessing of the Gentiles together with Israel, both in covenant relationship to God (v. 9b from 2 Sa 22:50 and Ps 18:49; v. 10 from Deu 32:43; v. 11 from Ps 117:1; v. 12 from Is 11:10). Paul certainly saw no theological teaching in the Old Testament that made any distinction between Jew and Gentile when both were in Christ. The Old Testament itself actually predicted the mutual acceptance of both on equal footing before God.

Finally, verse 13 forms a beautiful cornerstone to this whole section dealing with the relationship of Christians to one another. It is Paul's prayer for all believers that with the divine supply of joy and peace supplied to them through their continued faith, they might be strengthened by the power of the indwelling Spirit so that they can abound in the hope of their future final salvation.

In our day the church urgently needs Paul's insights and admonitions in this section. While a large segment of Christendom seeks unity on a false basis, we who confess Jesus as divine Lord divide ourselves from one another over the slightest differences. In many evangelical churches the weak have gained control and through extrabiblical rules and restrictions have rejected the strong from membership. Racial prejudice in varying degrees still abounds in many of our churches today.

Nevertheless, wherever Christians have been enabled to overcome these barriers that divide them, there is found the greatest testimony to the living Christ among His people. This is the Christian church's greatest glory. Not that it can penetrate to the most orthodox interpretation of Scriptures, though it is important to know what Scripture teaches, or delineate the best expression of what it means to have a Christian testimony today, but the church's greatest glory is that, in spite of strong differences among us, we can fully accept one another *even as* Christ also fully accepted us. It is not that the whole church holds one opinion, but that it follows one purpose and with one mouth of praise glorifies God.

From this section (14:1—15:13) we learn that faith-living for the Christian means doing whatever we do in conscious honoring

of the Lord (14:6). Sin, on the other hand, consists not in breaking the traditional taboos but more in a betrayal of our own faith
convictions (14:23), or in causing a brother to stumble by luring
him through our liberty to go against his own faith convictions
(14:15), or by passing any presumptive judgment on a brother in
any of these areas (14:10-12). Finally, the real glory of God is
manifested when we fully accept each other in spite of these
strong differences in convictions (15:7).

# 4

## *The Closing*

### 15:14—16:27

PAUL IS NOW FINISHED with the main body of his letter. The remainder of the materials entail words of a more personal nature, including his purpose in writing, encouragements, commendations, greetings, a final warning, and closing doxology. Our treatment will be brief, simply calling attention to some of the more significant features.

#### PAUL'S REASON FOR WRITING
#### 15:14-21

In this section Paul very tactfully relates his purpose for writing to the Romans. His somewhat bold letter to them was penned not so much to instruct them in new truth or to spoon-feed them, since he concedes that they were knowledgeable and able to instruct each other (v. 14) but to strongly remind them of these well-known truths and their implications (v. 15). This apostolic ministry to the Roman Gentiles is viewed by Paul as a "priestly" service to God. He offers up the evangelized Gentiles as his sacrificial offering (v. 16). This is a beautiful thought. Paul views his service in the gospel as an act of worship.

The apostle ascribes the glory for what has been done and said by him solely to Christ, though he has reason, humanly speaking, to be proud of his work (vv. 17-18). Christ's working through Paul also included miracles ("signs and wonders") as means of the Spirit's attestation of the truth of the gospel (v. 19; see also 2 Co 12:12; Gal 3:5; Heb 2:4).

"From Jerusalem . . . as far as Illyricum" (Dalmatia, northwest of Macedonia) sets the eastern and western limit where Paul had planted the gospel thus far in his ministry (v. 19). His activity was aimed at, though certainly not limited to, territories where no church was established (v. 20). This type of ministry Paul sees as a fulfillment of the prophecy of Isaiah (52:15) in foretelling of those who though ignorant of the Word of God would hear of the Messiah and respond (v. 21).

PAUL'S PERSONAL PLANS
15:22-33

Paul planned to go to Spain and make a stopover in Rome enroute (v. 24) after he had taken a special financial gift to the church in Jerusalem sent by the Christians in Macedonia and Achaia (v. 26). Like his statement in 1:13, he again assures them of his interest in visiting them even though until now he has been unable to come because of the busy schedule in fulfilling his primary evangelistic calling. He would, however, come and fellowship with them, and allow them to send him on his journey to Spain. Missionary and church were closely bound together.

Paul also takes time to describe the significance of the gift from the Gentiles to the Jews at Jerusalem (vv. 25-27). Since the Jews were the original stock of the Abrahamic covenant blessings, Gentiles who have become partakers in these "spiritual" blessings rightly feel an obligation to share with the Jews their "material" blessings (v. 27). The gifts are a seal and a fruit of the love and bond that exists between these brethren though they live in different parts of the world and are different culturally.

It is noteworthy how Paul regularly solicits the prayers of believers for his special needs and circumstances. He realizes that faces unfriendly to the gospel of Christ await him in Jerusalem. How much he needs the prayers of the saints for deliverance and prayer that the Jews would accept the Gentile gift and that at last he might indeed visit the Romans in God's will (vv. 30-33)! Paul trusted the Roman Christians and put great confidence in them.

It is instructive to trace the answer to Paul's prayer. Part of Paul's prayer was answered just as the joyous reception he received in Jerusalem (Ac 21:17-20); part was not answered exactly as he wished in that he was seized by the unbelieving Jews (though not harmed) and yet delivered from them by the Roman cohort (Ac 21:27, 32); part of his prayer was answered differently than he planned in that, although he went to Rome, he went under arrest (Ac 28:16); and part was answered much later on in his life when he was released from prison and apparently completed his tour to Spain on a final missionary journey (1 Ti 1:3; 2 Ti 4:13; Titus 1:5; 3:12.[1]

### COMMENDATION OF PHOEBE
### 16:1-2

On the northeastern side of the city of Corinth lay one of its ports, the city of Cenchrea. From a church located there came Phoebe who is described as a "servant" (Gk. *diakonos*) and a "helper [lit. protectress, patroness] of many," including Paul (v. 2). She may have been quite wealthy and socially prominent. It is difficult to argue convincingly that Phoebe was an official "deaconess" of her church. More likely she carried the letter of Paul to the Romans, and chapter 16 formed a necessary letter of commendation for her to the Roman Christians[2] (2 Co 3:1). This woman among a number of others like Prisca has been immortalized in the Christian tradition because of her deep dedication to Christ and the service she faithfully rendered to aid the gospel. Here is also one more glimpse into the radically transforming power of Christ to change a woman from paganism (Phoebe: "goddess of the moon") to a devoted and highly notable servant of Jesus Christ. Note also here and in the following verses the very high place women hold in the Christian mission. At least nine women are addressed in verses 1-16, and they are called "fellow-workers," not maid servants!

1. This is based on the inference that these letters were written after Paul's release from his first imprisonment and refer to places not mentioned in Acts as related to any of his first three missionary journeys.
2. See Introduction for a discussion of the problem of whether chapter 16 was part of the original letter.

## HELLOS TO PAUL'S FRIENDS
### 16:3-16

This section is a greatly neglected portion of Scripture, yet it provides a fascinating historical picture of the composition of a typical cross section of the early Christian church. There are no less than twenty-six different people greeted by Paul from all walks of life and background. Some are Jews (Prisca and Aquila, vv. 3-5), some names are Greek (Aristobulus, v. 10), others Roman (Rufus, v. 13; Urbanus, v. 9), some are women (Mary, v. 6; Julia, v. 15), some sisters (Tryphaena and Tryphosa, twins?, v. 12), a mother is mentioned (v. 13), prisoners (v. 7), relatives of Paul (vv. 7, 11), a family of a deceased man (Narcisussus, v. 11), and so on. Some were no doubt wealthy and noble; others were poor and slaves.

What does Paul say about these believers in Christ? He commends Aquila and his wife (Ac 18:1-3) for their service and courage in risking their lives for Paul (vv. 3-4). Epaenetus receives the title "my beloved" because he was the first convert from Asia (v. 5). Mary's hard work and industry are recalled (v. 6). Two Jewish believers, Andronicus and Junias, who knew Christ even before Paul was converted, are referred to as "outstanding among the apostles." Apelles is "approved in Christ," perhaps through trials (v. 10).

Rufus (v. 13) may well be the son of Simon of Cyrene who bore Jesus' cross (Mk 15:21). If so, it would show why Mark specifically mentioned his name and further connected the gospel of Mark with Rome. He is called "a choice man in the Lord" not because he was chosen to salvation but because he was selected for some special honor to which he was called by Christ. Rufus' mother became a mother also to Paul in some way. Paul may have lost his mother through death or because she never became a Christian. Perhaps Simon, the father, was saved, then the mother and the whole family.

In verse 14, Paul greets five men and a group who were with them. Could this be some type of early all-male Christian commune? Believers are further exhorted to greet one another with a "holy kiss" (Ro 16:16; see also 1 Co 16:20; 1 Th 5:26; 1 Pe 5:14).

Such a warm Christian token of love is conspicuous by its absence in the modern Western church.

In summary, we might learn some important things about effective Christian service from this chapter. First, Paul was interested in people. To him Christianity was persons following Jesus Christ. He may have had a long prayer list. Paul's commendations seem to highlight faithful labor as the predominant quality (Rev 2:2). He commended those he worked with and constantly held them up for recognition (12:10). Note also the high place of women in the service for Christ. Paul shows how important these ladies were to him for the advancement of the gospel. Finally, remember that the gospel of Christ when faithfully proclaimed and taught bears fruit in the lives of all kinds of people. This section illustrates in living stories the truth of Romans 1:16, "The gospel . . . it is the power of God unto salvation to *everyone* who believes."

## A FINAL WARNING
### 16:17-20

Before Paul's concluding remarks, he pauses to issue a direct warning against fellowshiping with those who taught doctrines contrary to the original apostolic teachings (v. 17). It is not exactly clear to whom Paul has reference. These deceivers may be the same crowd that created a problem for the churches of Galatia (Gal 3:1; 5:7, 20), Colosse (Col 2:20-23), and Philippi (Phil 3:19). "Slaves . . . of their own appetites [lit. belly]" (v. 18) probably does not refer to their physical appetites for food but their own self-centered, lustful living and preoccupation with food laws (Ja 3:15; Jude 19).

This heretical group should not be confused with the "weak" Christians of chapter 14 whom Paul exhorts to "accept" into the fellowships. It is vital to note this distinction lest we be "marking" fellow Christians who have different opinions as "deceivers." The "unsuspecting" are those who do not suspect any deception and therefore uncritically soak up the false teaching to their own harm.

Yet Paul is not insinuating that the Romans had actually fallen prey to this teaching; rather he commends them for their obedi-

ence and faithfulness (v. 19). Nevertheless the apostle wants
them to be alert to deception—"wise in what is good"—and un-
involved with any heresy or evil practice—"innocent [inexperi-
enced] in what is evil" (v. 19). This is a tremendously needed
balance in our lives: to know the good well enough to do it and
to know enough about error to be warned of its presence (e.g.,
drugs, demonism, occult, oriental mysticism, etc.), so we may
avoid experience with these things which damage our persons
and hinder our relationship with God. Grotius paraphrases, "Too
good to deceive, and too wise to be deceived."

Verse 20 contains an allusion to Genesis 3:15. It is Satan who
causes these heresies and allures men into their evil consequences,
but it is God who, in the soon coming of Jesus, will deal the final
death blow to Satan's activities. The hope of the final over-
coming of all enemies of Christ sustains believers in their present
battle against these forces (1 Co 15:25-28).

### Hellos from Paul's Companions
### 16:21-24

Timothy is well known (Ac 16:1-2). Lucias, Jason, and Sosi-
pater were probably Jewish relatives of Paul (see 16:7). Tertius
(v. 22) wrote the letter in the sense of serving as Paul's secretary
(amanuensis) which was the apostle's custom (1 Co 16:21; Col
4:18; 2 Th 3:17; Gal 6:11). Gaius hosted not only Paul but the
whole church at Corinth in his house! He must have had much
but also used it for the Lord. Gaius may be the same individual
referred to elsewhere as Titius Justus (1 Co 1:14; Ac 18:7; 19:29).

Erastus is called the "treasurer" of the city of Corinth. He
must have been a prominent man in Corinth. These men were
usually slaves, though wealthy (Ac 8:27). In 1931, a Latin inscription dated A.D. 50-100 was found at Corinth bearing the
name of Erastus who was honored because he paved a street.[3]
This might well have been the same man. The repeated benedic-
tions in verses 20 and 24 are by no means scribal slips but fitting
endings for each section.

---

3. H. J. Cadbury, "Erastus of Corinth," *Journal of Biblical Literature* 50
(1931):42-58.

## THE DOXOLOGY
### 16:25-27

Such a long doxology is not unfamiliar in the New Testament (Heb 13:20, 21; Jude 24, 25), though it is not customary for Paul.[4] It is a superb summary of the main notes of the epistle and in perfect harmony with its contents and with the teaching of other Pauline letters (Eph 3:20; 1 Ti 1:17). In particular, the significant strands of chapter one are picked up and reiterated in a beautiful concluding praise to God Himself.

The apostle begins with reference to the strengthening power of God granted to believers and resulting from the ministry of Paul's preaching of the gospel of Jesus Christ (1:11). This gospel of Paul's is in fact a "revelation of the mystery which has been kept secret for long ages past" (lit. in eternal times). On Paul's use of the term "mystery" see discussion at 11:25. Here the content of the mystery is much broader. It is not certain whether by the expression, "for long ages past," Paul means, "since the creation began" (see 2 Ti 1:9; Titus 1:2), or "in the eternal times of God." Perhaps the term means "times reaching back to eternity."[5] In any case, the mystery of the gospel of Jesus Christ, God's Son (1:3, 4), which was kept quiet in the past, is now fully revealed to all men: "But now is manifested" (v. 26).

Paul links this present gospel revelation to the "Scriptures of the prophets." How the mystery which has been hid in the past can now be revealed in Scripture, which has been known for centuries, presents a problem. One solution posits the view that the phrase "Scripture of the prophets" refers to the New Testament prophets and the apostolic Scriptures (2 Pe 3:16).[6] Yet it is difficult to maintain this view in light of Paul's abundant quotation of Scripture in Romans all taken only from the Old Testament; the parallel in 1:2 certainly refers to Old Testament; and in light of the early date of this epistle (before A.D. 60) very little New Testament Scripture would have been written. It seems best to

---

4. On the textual problem of this section and the general integrity problem of chapters 15-16, see Introduction.
5. E. H. Gifford, "Romans" in *The Bible Commentary,* p. 237.
6. See F. L. Godet, *Commentary on the Epistle to the Romans* (Grand Rapids: Zondervan, 1969), and James M. Stifler, *The Epistle to the Romans* (Chicago: Moody, 1960), for a defense of this view.

maintain a tension between what was revealed in promise in the Old Testament concerning the gospel and which belonged primarily to Israel and what is now revealed in history in Jesus Christ and by the command of the eternal God made known (and thus given) to all peoples. This mystery is not an esoteric phenomenon which is the property of an elite few, but God commands that the knowledge is to be given without distinction through the Scriptures to all men in order to bring them to the "obedience of faith" in Jesus Christ.

Paul began his doxology with an address to the one who is *able* to establish us; and now, after contemplating the tremendous mystery of the gospel, he closes by turning to the "only wise God" (v. 27). To this God of unfathomable wisdom, the one who has revealed the mystery of His plan for the salvation of the whole created order effected through Jesus Christ, Paul can only attribute eternal glory.[7] Amen!

Thus, as the epistle began with the promise of God (1:2-4), so it ends with the glory of God. The letter is perhaps the greatest treatise that has ever been written concerning God.[8]

---

7. It is not clear whether Paul meant to attribute the glory to Christ or to the Father in this last statement. While it would be appropriate to address this to Jesus Christ (2 Pe 3:18; Rev 1:6; 5:12, 13), since the opening words of the doxology are addressed to the Father ("to the only wise God"). it may be better to refer the latter also to Him.

8. Leon Morris, "The Theme of Romans" in *Apostolic History and the Gospel,* ed. W. Ward Gasque and Ralph P. Martin, p. 263.

# Selected Bibliography

SINCE GOOD COMMENTARIES on Romans abound, it may be more helpful to list some worthy volumes in several categories, with brief comments, than to multiply titles. Unless otherwise noted, the writers are conservative and evangelical in theology.

### BROAD OVERVIEW AND SYNTHESIS

Erdman, Charles. *The Epistle of Paul to the Romans.* Philadelphia: Westminster, 1925. Best for summarizing the overall content of each section and tracing the logical argument.

Liddon, H. P. *An Explanatory Analysis of St. Paul's Epistle to the Romans.* Grand Rapids: Zondervan, 1961. Excellent on the logical point-by-point progression, in outline form with notes. Quite detailed and technical. Good historical material.

Ridenour, Fritz. *How to Be a Christian Without Being Religious.* Glendale: Gospel Light: Regal, 1967. Very popular treatment involving *The Living Bible* paraphrase with general comments in modern language, with illustrations. Not much depth but a good light introduction to Romans.

Spivey, Robert A. and Smith, D. Moody Jr. *Anatomy of the New Testament.* Rev. ed. New York: Macmillan, 1974. Not a conservative book but highly commendable for putting the chief content of Romans into historical perspective for more advanced students.

Stifler, James M. *The Epistle to the Romans.* Chicago: Moody, 1960. Good on tracing the thought progression and general content. More detailed than Erdman above.

### EXEGETICAL AND INTERPRETIVE

Barrett, C. K. *The Epistle to the Romans.* New York: Harper & Row, 1957. Not thoroughly conservative but close to the biblical text and one of the best in this category.

Bruce, F. F. *The Epistle of Paul to the Romans.* Grand Rapids: Eerdmans, 1963. Good treatment of almost all verses with help in the area of historical illustration materials.

Cranfield, C. E. B. *A Critical and Exegetical Commentary on the Epistle to the Romans.* The International Critical Commentary. 2 vols. Edinburgh: T. & T. Clark, 1975, 1979 The best, more-detailed critical study available in English. For advanced students. A rich mine of interpretive help.

Gifford, E. H. "Romans." In *The Bible Commentary: New Testament,* vol. 3. Ed. F. C. Cook. New York: Scribners, 1895. Old and out of print but still one of the best careful treatments of the thought and details.

Mickelsen, Berkeley. "Romans." In *Wycliffe Bible Commentary.* Charles F. Pfeiffer and Everett F. Harrison. Chicago: Moody, 1962. An excellent brief exposition and interpretation by a leading evangelical scholar.

Murray, John. *The Epistle to the Romans.* 2 vols. Grand Rapids: Eerdmans, 1959. Easily one of the best treatments on the book. Careful, evangelical, and detailed.

Nygren, Anders. *Commentary on Romans.* Philadelphia: Fortress, 1949. A powerful treatment of the epistle by a Lutheran theologian. Very helpful on main argument of book. Not thoroughly evangelical.

OTHER SUGGESTIONS

Jones, Alexander, gen. ed. *The Jerusalem Bible.* New York: Doubleday, 1966. Produced by Dominican Catholics in Jerusalem and containing in Romans, with a few exceptions, some excellent notes and fresh insights on the text.

Kittel, Gerhard and Friedrich, G. ed. *Theological Dictionary of the New Testament.* Trans. Geoffrey W. Bromiley. 9 vols. Grand Rapids: Eerdmans, 1964. An unabridged English translation for advanced students with some Greek background. Rather heavy but when used with theological discrimination it is a valuable resource for interpreting Romans. (Referred to in the text and notes of this book as TDNT.)